Essential Series

Springer

London
Berlin
Heidelberg
New York
Hong Kong
Milan
Paris
Tokyo

Also in this series:

John Cowell
Essential Visual Basic 5.0 *fast*
3-540-76148-9

Duncan Reed and Peter Thomas
Essential HTML *fast*
3-540-76199-3

John Vince
Essential Virtual Reality *fast*
1-85233-012-0

John Cowell
Essential Visual J++ 6.0 *fast*
1-85233-013-9

John Cowell
Essential Java 2 *fast*
1-85233-071-6

John Cowell
Essential Visual Basic 6.0 *fast*
1-85233-071-6

John Vince
Essential Computer Animation *fast*
1-85233-141-0

Aladdin Ayesh
Essential Dynamic HTML *fast*
1-85233-626-9

David Thew
Essential Access 2000 *fast*
1-85233-295-6

Ian Palmer
Essential Java 3D *fast*
1-85233-394-4

Matthew Norman
Essential ColdFusion *fast*
1-85233-315-4

Ian Chivers
Essential Linux *fast*
1-85233-408-8

Fiaz Hussain
Essential Flash 5.0 *fast*
1-85233-451-7

John Vince
Essential Mathematics for
Computer Graphics *fast*
1-85233-380-4

John Cowell
Essential VB .NET *fast*
1-85233-591-2

Simon Stobart
Essential PHP *fast*
1-85233-578-5

Fiaz Hussain
Essential Dreamweaver 4.0 *fast*
1-85233-573-4

Aladdin Ayesh
Essential UML *fast*
1-85233-413-4

Simon Stobart
Essential ASP .NET *fast*
1-85233-683-8

John Cowell
Essential XHTML *fast*
1-85233-684-6

Ian Stephenson

Essential RenderMan® *fast*

 Springer

Ian Stephenson, DPhil
National Centre for Computer Animation, Bournemouth University, Poole
BH12 5BB, UK

Series Editor
John Cowell, BSc (Hons), MPhil, PhD
Department of Computer Science, De Montfort University, The Gateway,
Leicester LE1 9BH

British Library Cataloguing in Publication Data
Stephenson, Ian
    Essential RenderMan fast. – (Essential series)
    1. RenderMan (Computer file) 2. Computer graphics 3. Computer
    animation
    I. Title II. RenderMan fast
    006.6
    ISBN 1852336080

Library of Congress Cataloging-in-Publication Data
A catalog record for this book is available from the Library of Congress

Essential series ISSN 1439-975X

ISBN 1-85233-608-0 Springer-Verlag London Berlin Heidelberg
a member of BertelsmannSpringer Science+Business Media GmbH
http://www.springer.co.uk

Back cover image of Aki, from Final Fantasy, © 2001 FFFP

Typesetting: Mac Style Ltd, Scarborough, N. Yorkshire
Printed and bound at The Cromwell Press, Trowbridge, Wiltshire
34/3830-543210 Printed on acid-free paper SPIN 10874087

Acknowledgements

Big thanks to everyone at the NCCA, both staff and students, but extra special mentions to John Vince for suggesting I do this, and John Haddon for asking me so many incredibly insightful stupid questions that I couldn't get away with anything. This book owes a lot to the students and ex-students who have attended my RenderMan workshops during the last few years. The Robot and Bear RIB files were originally created by Faan van Tonder and Frederic Cervini during those classes. It also wouldn't have been the same without Rob – even though he never got to read it.

Further afield Seamus and Dave at Techimage Ltd kept me fed with various pieces of software, which made the whole thing technically possible. Lots of credit must also go to Pixar, DotC Software (Rick and Cheryl), Sitex Graphics (Scott), Exluna, ART and the other renderer developers for giving me something to talk about. RenderMan is a trademark of Pixar.

Jerome Dewhurst photographed the environment map of Lightsite studios in London, while the other texture maps were photographed by Amanda Rochfort. Thanks to Kevin Bjorke and Square USA for the Final Fantasy image.

Finally, a confession to Pete, Rog and everyone else in the Adaptive Systems Lab at the University of York in the early 1990s. I guess it's now pretty obvious who stole the group's copy of the *RenderMan Companion*. Sorry guys – if it's any consolation, I think I put it to good use.

Contents

Contents

Part

1

General Overview

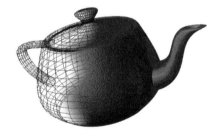

Chapter

1

What is RenderMan?

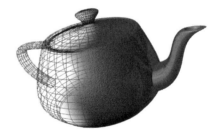

If you're reading this it is probably because someone showed you some work and told you it was "rendered with RenderMan". Perhaps you saw *Toy Story* or *Monsters Inc.* and decided to find out more about the RenderMan software used to create it. In fact, nothing was ever rendered with RenderMan, and RenderMan isn't even a piece of software. It therefore seems essential that the first thing that should be established is what exactly RenderMan is.

RenderMan is a rendering API. What this means in practice is that RenderMan defines how animation and modelling software, such as SoftImage or Maya, should talk to rendering software, as in Figure 1.1. The rendering software receives instructions from the modeller that describe the scene and from these commands it generates images. This separation of modelling from rendering benefits developers of modellers, developers of renderers, and end users.

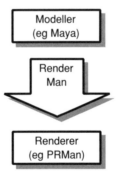

Figure 1.1 A rendering API.

The API was developed by Pixar in the late 1980s at a time when they were developing custom rendering hardware. They were concerned that as wide a range of users as possible should be able to make use of their hardware, and hence entered into discussion with other major graphics companies. The result of these negotiations was the publication of the RenderMan standard. The idea was that anyone could develop modelling software which could talk to Pixar's new hardware. In addition anyone could build a rendering system which conformed to the standard – the standard being designed to avoid being directly linked to any particular renderer. Any modeller that conformed to the standard, would be able to render its images using any renderer that conformed to the standard.

Ideally, users would be able to select the modeller that best suited their needs, and match it to a renderer with an appropriate set of features, as in Figure 1.2. Software developers could focus on the area of the animation pipeline in which they excelled, and let others provide the tools required for other tasks. Technical directors who developed skills in RenderMan would be able to apply their expertise even when their employer upgraded to a different software package.

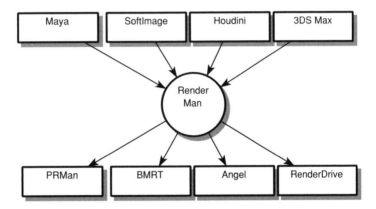

Figure 1.2 Mix and match toolsets.

Unfortunately, owing to the politics of commercial production and software development, this situation did not materialize. Pixar's hardware failed to become commercially viable, though they did produce a very successful software implementation of their renderer which also conformed to the RenderMan standard. This software is known as PhotoRealistic RenderMan, or PRMan. However, for many years no other RenderMan compliant renderers were available. In fact, RenderMan became synonymous with PRMan.

Though the PRMan software has always been considered to be excellent, it is rather expensive. Only a few companies producing high quality film work could afford PRMan, and as a result few modelling packages made the effort to provide good support for RenderMan renderers. This catch-22 situation persisted for most of the 1990s.

Things began to change with the release of Blue Moon Rendering Tools (BMRT). When this renderer was made available at very low cost, RenderMan became available to a new group of users who could never have gained access to PRMan. Since then, many renders that claim some degree of RenderMan compatibility have become available. Each of these provides a different set of strengths and features such as global illumination, speed, portability or simply cost. Many of these renderers are commercial, while others are available as free downloads from the authors' websites.

Support in animation packages is still improving. Some packages, such as Houdini, have good support for RenderMan renderers built in, but most require a plug-in of some kind. The style and quality of these plug-ins varies, as does their cost and availability.

At the time of writing we are finally getting close to the original Pixar idea of RenderMan everywhere. Ten years after the original publication of the original RenderMan standard Pixar have released the long-awaited 3.2 revision of the RenderMan standard document. Many production houses are using high quality RenderMan compliant renderers, and RenderMan is at last starting to realize its potential as the PostScript of 3D.

Further information

A formal history of the RenderMan API written by two of its key architects, Ed Catmull and Pat Hanrahan, can be found in the Foreword to the *RenderMan Companion*. A slightly less reverent version forms the Afterword to *Advanced RenderMan* and answers the question: "Why the name 'RenderMan'?"

Chapter 2

Is RenderMan for Me?

Rendering is a complex part of the computer imaging process. RenderMan gives the user control over almost all aspects of this process and hence a full understanding can take many years to acquire. To use a RenderMan renderer to its full potential on a project requires the same investment in time and effort as you might expect to spend learning an animation and modelling package. Fortunately, it is possible to gain substantial benefits from a more limited effort.

This book assumes no specific knowledge of rendering, but some background experience of computer graphics techniques is useful. Limited programming experience is required but in most cases the complexity of code required to produce useful results is far simpler than found in even the most basic programming books and courses – most of our programs will be ten lines of code or less. Similarly, the mathematics of rendering can be somewhat involved, but most of this is hidden within the rendering system itself. This book is aimed at a user who may not yet be technically skilled but is prepared to become more involved in technical issues in order to produce images of the highest quality.

In principle, it should be possible to use a RenderMan compliant renderer from a compatible animation package with virtually no knowledge of the rendering API which is being used. In practice, however, this is rarely the case, and at the very least an understanding of the general architecture is invaluable. Though we'd like to be able to treat rendering as something that "just works", even the best rendering systems benefit from a little user intervention.

While the full details of the RenderMan API are complex, the structure is simple and a new user can rapidly gain enough experience to make minor modifications to scenes which have been generated by other means, for example changing the colour of an object, or re-rendering a scene at a higher resolution. Manually modifying a scene can enable access to the more powerful facilitates available in the renderer that may not be supported by a particular animation package, and inspecting the scenes generated by your modeller prior to rendering is a powerful debugging technique.

Users with more programming experience should be able to generate scenes from their own programs within a few weeks, allowing the development of custom modelling software without worrying about how the images will be rendered. A powerful production technique is to write programs that read in scenes via the RenderMan API, modify them, and write them out again. This allows a pipeline to be constructed which is independent of both modeller and renderer.

RenderMan's most powerful feature is the control it gives over the appearance of surfaces. Virtually any kind of surface texture, shading or deformation can be requested, and applied to any object. Defining high quality surfaces can be a complex task, taking in physics, mathematics, programming and aesthetic considerations, but in most cases the requirements of a particular surface for a single shot are far simpler, and even a novice user can produce interesting results with a little practice.

Chapter 3

An Overview of the RenderMan System

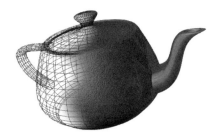

When the RenderMan standard was first proposed, computer graphics was still an esoteric topic of research practised by skilled proponents. The typical expectation was that these users would be writing their own programs to generate geometry, probably in the C programming language. As a result, the first release of the RenderMan API defined a set of C functions which could be called by modelling programs to pass instructions to a renderer.

While the C API is an appropriate mechanism for researchers to use when communicating to a renderer, it rapidly became clear that for commercial production, a more flexible mechanism was required. A modelling program should probably not be directly linked to a particular renderer. A scene may be generated on one platform, and then passed to a render farm to generate the images. For this reason the RIB (RenderMan Interface Byte stream) file format was introduced.

A modelling program will still make calls to the C API, but rather than actually rendering, these will typically write a RIB file to disk. These RIB files can then be examined, modified and finally passed to a stand-alone rendering program, perhaps running on a completely different machine.

The interface between the modeller and the renderer is therefore typically in the form of a RIB file. As a result, it is probably reasonable to say that the RIB file format represents the RenderMan standard – a RenderMan compliant modeller writes RIBs while a RenderMan compliant renderer reads RIBs.

While it is perfectly possible to simply rely on a modelling package to generate RIBs, a great deal of power and flexibility can be gained from even limited knowledge of the RIB format. RIB files are generally stored as text and can easily be created or modified by a user. Though they do tend to contain rather a lot of numbers representing points in 3D space which are hard to interpret manually, the overall structure consists of a list of simple commands which can easily be identified and understood.

Though RIBs define the geometry of a scene, RenderMan distinguishes between the shape of an object and its surface detail. Most objects are geometrically simple, and can be represented by very primitive geometry. For example, an orange is basically a sphere. However, real objects differ from stereotypical computer-generated objects in that on closer examination they display complex surface textures, and interact with light in a range of interesting fashions. A real orange is not perfectly round, it has pitting in the skin and an interesting waxy reaction to light.

While most modern rendering systems make some limited provision for modifying the surface properties of an object, the RenderMan standard goes further by defining a highly complex and flexible system where the surface properties of an object can be modified by "Shaders". Shaders take the form of short pieces of computer code written in a RenderMan specific language called SL – short for Shading Language. A renderer will typically be supplied with a program to convert shaders into a format which that particular renderer can use. This is known as the shader compiler.

When a surface is defined in a RIB file it is simply marked as having a particular shader attached. When the scene is rendered, the renderer will look for a compiled version of that shader, and use the code contained within it to calculate the appearance of the surface. It is this ability to have such fine control over the appearance of a surface which makes RenderMan renderers so powerful. On major projects which use RenderMan the job of shader writer may fully occupy several highly skilled members of the production crew. An understanding of shader writing is the key component in claiming to be able to "use RenderMan".

The full RenderMan pipeline can therefore be summarized by Figure 3.1.

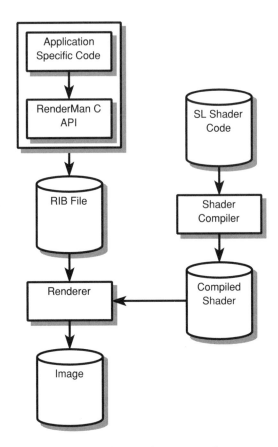

Figure 3.1 *The RenderMan pipeline.*

Chapter

4

What Do I Need?

The computing system used by Pixar to render their film *Monsters Inc.*, had over 3000 Sun SPARC CPUs, and is one of the most powerful clusters in existence. Just to purchase software licences for such a system would cost over $1 million. At the other end of the scale, however, most of the images in this book have been rendered using Angel on a 66 MHz 486 with 32 Mb of RAM running Windows NT, and a P133 with 40 Mb of RAM running Linux. A faster machine will reduce the time you have to wait, and more expensive software may generate a better-looking image, but the rendering process is otherwise identical. The information in this book applies equally to all the renderers, except where noted.

While having access to modelling software capable of interacting with RenderMan will be helpful, it is not necessary in order to make use of this book.

Hardware

RenderMan-compatible software is available for most types of computer. Traditionally, SGI workstations have been used for the kind of high end work that RenderMan is associated with, but renderers running under both Linux and Windows have become available in recent years. The underlying hardware and operating system has little direct impact on the rendering process though the scripting, and networking facilities of the UNIX-based systems still make them the preferred choice for experienced users.

The rendering process is a CPU-intensive task, which is little affected by other parameters of the machine it is running on. A fast CPU is therefore a major asset, but all of the scenes in this book may be rendered in a reasonable amount of time on current hardware. As the complexity of scenes increases, more memory may be required to render the scene efficiently. Memory can be particularly critical for ray tracers such as BMRT, but this should not be a problem when simply learning about the API. In extreme cases where very large scenes are being rendered on multiple machines, network architecture and disk input/output (i/o) bandwidth become significant issues but these are of little concern to the new user.

Though the machine used to generate the images simply requires CPU power and memory, at some point you are going to view the images produced on screen. To do this a 24 bit graphics card is almost essential. While a lower depth card may give a rough idea as to the general layout of the image, any fine detail will be lost, making quality work impossible.

Rendering software

In order to work through the examples in this book and to produce your own images, you will need a RenderMan-compliant renderer. Exactly which one is right for you depends on the needs and budget of the work you are aiming to produce. Fortunately, one of the key things about RenderMan is that you can start small, learn a little, and then switch software as required. RenderMan provides a common API, so when you learn to use one of these renderers you are learning about all the others too.

This section is by its very nature going to be out of date as soon as it is written, but it should give some indication of the kind of software that is available and what you can expect to get from each package. I apologize to the authors of any packages I have missed.

PhotoRealistic RenderMan (PRMan)

Written by Pixar this is the renderer which is most commonly associated with the name RenderMan. PRMan is extremely fast, and highly reliable, producing excellent quality results, as seen in movies such as *Toy Story* and *A Bug's Life*. It is based on a rendering technique known as REYES, and as such provides no facilities for global illumination, though a future version incorporating these features has been announced. Novice users find this something of a shock as they expect high-end software to handle reflections and shadows automatically. However, professional users are happy to trade these features for the flexibility and speed of the REYES approach. The quality of the system is reflected in its price of several thousand dollars.

The renderer is invoked with the command "render" on UNIX systems, and the command "prman" on Windows systems. Shaders are compiled using the command "shader", and compiled shaders have the file extension ".slo".

PRMan is available for SGI, Sun, DEC Alpha, Linux and Windows systems. Details are available from www.pixar.com.

RenderDotC

This renderer is in many ways similar to PRMan, in terms of feature set, performance and price. A broadcast version (with limited output resolution) is also available for a very competitive price. This has led to its adoption by a number of video production houses.

The renderer is invoked with the command "renderdc". Shaders are compiled using the command "shaderdc". Rather than storing compiled shaders in a proprietary file format, shaders are converted to C++ code, then compiled to a shared library ("so", or "dll" depending on the platform).

RenderDotC is available for SGI, Linux, HP and Windows systems. Further information and a resolution restricted demonstration version may be obtained from www.dotcsw.com.

ART RenderDrive

Rather than being a piece of software, the RenderDrive is a custom rendering device manufactured by Advanced

Rendering Technology Ltd which accepts RIB files and outputs frames. Instead of building a render farm from standard computers which require constant administration and maintenance, a production house may simply purchase a number of RenderDrive units, and connect them to the network. Animators then send their RIB files to the RenderDrive, and receive image files back.

By performing ray intersections in hardware the RenderDrive is able to produce ray traced scenes of exceedingly high quality far more quickly than would be possible with conventional hardware. As such it has proved successful in the visualization and product design markets where the aim is to find out what something will look like before it is built.

Details are available from www.art-render.com.

AIR

AIR is a fast hybrid renderer, combining the speed of scanline rendering (for fast rendering of complex scenes, motion blur and depth of field) with the flexibility of ray tracing (for indirect illumination, accurate reflections and soft shadows).

The AIR renderer is invoked by the "air" command on Windows or Linux. Shaders are compiled with the shading compiler "shaded" to .slb files. A shader can be compiled to machine code for faster execution by passing a -dll or -dso option to the shading compiler.

An evaluation of AIR is available from http://www.sitexgraphics.com

Blue Moon Rendering Tools (BMRT)

One of the oldest RenderMan-compliant renderers, this renderer was made freely available by its author, Larry Gritz. The product itself is an excellent ray tracer and radiosity renderer, though it is not intended to be used as a full production renderer. The low cost and strong feature set has made BMRT one of the most widely used RenderMan renderers, giving many users their first access to RenderMan. Its performance is slightly sluggish, though this is to be expected, considering the facilities it provides. It has often been used in commercial productions to provide global illumination facilities for users who would otherwise rely on PRMan.

Running on Sun, DEC Alpha, Linux, SGI and Windows, scenes are rendered by the "rendrib" command, and shaders compiled with "slc" to produce ".slc" files.

BMRT is available for free download from www.exluna.com.

Entropy

Having worked for Pixar for a number of years, a number of developers created Exluna, with the aim of developing rendering and texturing tools. Their first commercial product – Entropy – is a descendant of BMRT, but includes many improvements, enabling it to handle the huge scenes required by modern film production.

Details of Entropy are available from www.exluna.com.

Aqsis

Aqsis is an Open Source REYES style renderer, currently running under Windows. It is free, and relatively fast. These features make it a good choice for getting to grips with RenderMan.

Source and executables for Aqsis are available from www.sourceforge.com. Further information is on www.maxdepth.demon.co.uk.

Angel

Angel is a lightweight Z-Buffer renderer. As such it is suitable for rendering tests, though it is not designed as a production renderer. It is freely available for Linux, freeBSD, SGI and Windows from www.dctsystems.freeserve.co.uk.

Scenes are rendered with the command "angel", while the shader compiler "giles" is designed to be compatible with BMRT and produces ".slc" files.

Summary

As RenderMan is an API rather than a renderer, it is available in a range of forms to suit virtually every kind of user. All of these renderers should be able to render all of the examples used in this book, with a few minor exceptions. If you are able to install more than one, this will allow you to compare their relative merits, and help you understand how RenderMan makes working with multiple renderers (and modellers) practical.

Production notes, detailing specific issues which might arise as you work through this book using some of the renderers listed above are available from the Essentials website.

Chapter 5

How to Use this Book

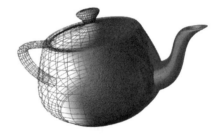

This book is divided into three parts. Part 1 you've already read, and gives a general overview of the RenderMan architecture. By now you should have a good idea how the various parts of RenderMan fit together, and how it fits within a production pipeline. The remaining two parts discuss the creation of geometry and shading.

Part 2 considers geometry. We start with a simple five-line RIB file, and learn how to specify increasingly complex objects, from spheres and cones, through to complex free-form surfaces, hair and particle systems. Once you've got to grips with RIB, you'll learn how this knowledge can be used from the C programming language. In addition to the actual shape of the objects themselves, Part 2 also includes details of how colours and shaders are attached to objects, how the camera is setup, and information on lighting your scene.

Part 3 considers the second part of the RenderMan API – the writing of shaders. Initially we look at how the standard shaders operate, and progress by adding increasingly complex patterns to our surfaces. We examine how objects may be given a more organic feel, through the use of noise, and use displacement shaders to emboss patterns onto objects. The topic of anti-aliasing is discussed; we develop surfaces which interact with light in unique ways, and new kinds of lights which shine light in interesting patterns.

Though there is necessarily an overlap between Parts 2 and 3, it should be possible to read each part independently. If you are interested in generating or modifying geometry you can read only Part 2, while if you want to learn about shader writing quickly then you can skip ahead to Part 3, referring back to Part 2 as required.

Both Parts 2 and 3 include numerous worked examples. Having read each chapter, you should render the examples contained within it using at least one compliant renderer. All of the code in the book can be obtained from the Essential series website at www.essential-series.com. The examples should be modified to verify their behaviour, and explore the ideas introduced. Suggestions are made at the end of each chapter as to how the techniques you've learnt might be applied. These should be considered carefully to gain maximum benefit from the chapter.

This book is not intended to provide an exhaustive reference to the RenderMan API. It is intended as a tutorial, giving you a start into the RenderMan world. It introduces the concepts, and shows you how to make use of them in a practical fashion. In many cases there are additional options or subtleties which are ignored for the sake of clarity. Each chapter includes a section describing some of the related commands and functions which you might like to find out more about. Details of these commands along with other more general information on rendering can be found in a number of more advanced books which are listed in the bibliography. These can be referred to for more technically detailed information, once you're comfortable with the basic ideas.

Part

2

Geometry

Geometry is presented to the renderer either through a RIB file or C API. These are closely related, and once you have learnt one, it is relatively simple to use the other. However, as the issues of C programming would only make the discussion of RenderMan more complex, we will at first restrict ourselves to using RIB. The C API will be briefly introduced in a latter section, on the basis that proficient programmers will be able to cope with the required leap.

Rather than attempt to cover each class of commands in turn, and provide a full reference, we'll start with a simple scene and extend it, introducing new concepts and commands as they seem appropriate. The details of many commands will be omitted, as they may easily be looked up in the reference texts.

The API will be introduced by a series of increasingly complex examples. Each listing will be accompanied by a figure, so the code and resultant image can easily be compared. Each chapter concludes with a list of related commands which are more complex to use, or simply less useful. These are intended as suggestions for further study which you can choose to investigate or ignore as required.

You should attempt to render and extend the examples in each chapter, as this is the only method by which familiarity can be gained with the rendering process. Except where noted, all the examples should work equally well regardless of the renderer you use.

Chapter

6

A Simple Scene

Introduction

Perhaps the hardest part of using any package is actually producing your first image. In this section we'll produce a simple scene by creating a RIB file and passing it to a renderer. In doing so, you'll learn about the basic structure of a RIB file, and gain the practical experience needed to progress further. This will form the basis of the more complex examples in later chapters.

Making a RIB

RIB files for high-quality frames can be several gigabytes in size, but more basic images can be produced with only a few bytes. In production, RIB files are often stored in a non-human readable format to save disk space, but for our purposes we can simply store RIBs as text files. One of the simplest possible scenes is a single sphere in the centre of the screen. The RIB for this is in Listing 6.1, and the resultant image is shown in Figure 6.1.

Listing 6.1 A minimal scene.

```
#min.rib - a minimal scene
Display "min.tiff" "file" "rgb"
Projection "perspective"
WorldBegin
    Translate 0 0 2
    Sphere 1 -1 1 360
WorldEnd
```

Figure 6.1 A minimal scene.

The RIB file contains a list of commands for the renderer. Typically these will be positioned at the start of a line, and may be followed by a number of parameters. These parameters are separated by spaces, and may be split across several lines if necessary to make the file more readable. Throughout Part 2 of this book we'll look at increasingly complex commands, and see how they can be combined together to create interesting scenes.

You should type this RIB into the computer using any text editor (such as NotePad.exe, VI or Emacs) and save it to disk. Though any file name could be used, as this is one of the smallest possible RIB files we'll call it "min.rib"

What goes in a RIB?

We'll now examine the contents of min.rib.

#comment

Anything which follows a # character up until the end of line, is ignored by the renderer. You can therefore use that space to add any information which might be useful to someone reading the RIB file. In this case we've added a line which includes the name of the file, and a brief description of the scene's contents.

Display

The real work of this RIB file starts with a `Display` command indicating that we want to create a file called min.tiff, containing RGB (red green blue) colour information. As an alternative, replacing "file" with "framebuffer" would display the image directly on the screen.

Projection

The line beginning `Projection` simply tells the renderer that we want to use a standard perspective projection – far away things will be drawn smaller than close up things. A particular renderer may support other projections, but most rendering uses this standard projection.

WorldBegin and WorldEnd

Having set up the renderer, telling it how to draw, and where to store the results, we can start telling it about the things to be drawn. The command `WorldBegin` informs the renderer that the set-up phase is complete, and it should prepare to draw. The related command at the end of the file `WorldEnd` informs it that the scene is finished, and it can write out the final image.

Translate and Sphere

Between WorldBegin and WorldEnd we define the objects that we want in our scene. In this case we have a single sphere, declared with the Sphere command, and positioned using the Translate command. Both of these will be covered in greater detail in the following chapters.

Rendering a RIB

Having created a RIB file which describes a simple scene, we now want to turn the RIB into an image by rendering it. Most rendering is done from the command line rather than from a GUI so open a command prompt or shell and change to the directory in which you've created min.rib. It should then be possible to render the scene by simply typing the render command followed by the name of the RIB file.

The command needed to render the scene depends on the renderer you're using. Refer to Chapter 4 and the documentation for your renderer to check what this command should be. Some of the more common examples would be:

PRMan (unix)	render min.rib
PRMan (windows)	prman min.rib
BMRT	rendrib min.rib
Angel	angel min.rib

If all goes well then the file "min.tiff" should be created, and can be viewed using the image viewer of your choice. Depending on the renderer some diagnostics may also be printed, but for a successful render these are typically minimal.

Troubleshooting

If the file min.tiff is not created then something has gone wrong. A likely cause is simply that the rendering command has not been found. Check that you are using the correct command for your renderer, and that the renderer is correctly installed. You may need to set up the PATH environment variable to tell the shell where the renderer is installed.

If the render is being found, check that the file min.rib exists and is in the current directory. The current directory should also be write-enabled so that the image file can be created.

If these do not solve the problem then you are probably getting an error message from the renderer such as "Unknown Keyword", "Unknown Token" or "Parse Error". These indicate an error in the RIB file, and may also give a line number. Check that you have entered the RIB file correctly.

Suggested activities

Render min.rib using at least one RenderMan-compliant renderer. If you have more than one renderer available then try it in as many as possible and observe any differences. Modify it so that it outputs the image directly to the screen.

Summary

```
#This is a comment
Display "filename" "outputType" "rgb"
Projection "perspective"
WorldBegin
WorldEnd
```

Chapter 7

Moving Things Around

Introduction

Having created a basic framework for our scene we need to be able to orient and position objects within it. In this chapter we'll see how you can use transformations to move objects, resize them and rotate them, both individually and in groups.

Positioning objects

The RIB file defines a 3D world which initially is empty. The first thing within that world is the camera, and the position of everything else is specified in terms of its relationship to that camera. In "min.rib" we created a single sphere, and in order for it not to be in exactly the same place as the camera, we had to move it using a `Translate` command. The command used in min.rib was `Translate 0 0 2` indicating that the sphere was moved 0 units right, 0 units up and 2 units into the screen.

`Translate` is one of a number of commands known as transforms, which are used to position objects. These apply to everything that follows them, so the `Translate` command in min.rib appears before the `Sphere` command, which is on the following line. We could move the sphere left by adding the command `Translate -1 0 0` after the current `Translate` and before the `Sphere` as shown in Listing 7.1 and Figure 7.1. The two `Translate` are both applied so that the sphere is moved both two units back, and one unit left.

Listing 7.1 Moving objects around.

```
#left.rib
Display "left.tiff" "file" "rgb"
Projection "perspective"

WorldBegin
    #move everything back 2 units
    Translate 0 0 2
```

```
    #Everything that follows is one unit left
    Translate -1 0 0
    Sphere 1 -1 1 360
WorldEnd
```

Figure 7.1 *Moving objects around.*

If you wanted to display two spheres, you could do so using the commands shown in Listing 7.2, which uses a Translate to place the first sphere on the left, and a second Translate to move the second sphere right. However, Figure 7.2 shows that rather than displaying one sphere on the left and the other on the right as might be expected, this displays one on the left and one in the centre. The thing we've overlooked is that transforms apply to everything that follows them, so the first Translate moves the first sphere to the left but it also moves the second sphere left, and the Translate right only moves it back as far as the middle.

Listing 7.2 Multiple transforms.

```
#transform.rib
Display "transform.tiff" "file" "rgb"
Projection "perspective"
```

```
WorldBegin
    #move everything back 2 units
    Translate 0 0 2

    #Everything that follows is one unit left
    Translate -1 0 0
    Sphere 1 -1 1 360

    #Everything that follows is one unit right
    Translate 1 0 0
    Sphere 1 -1 1 360
WorldEnd
```

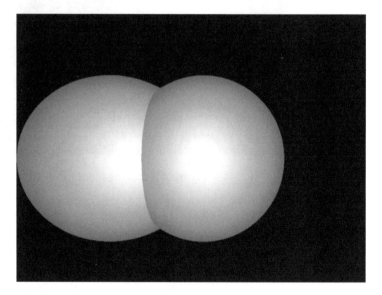

Figure 7.2 Multiple transforms.

Grouping transforms

While it would be possible to simply use Translate 2 0 0
to move the second sphere further right, this would be
tedious and difficult to keep track of in more complex scenes.
If you were to reposition the first sphere you would have to
adjust the second translation to keep the second sphere still.

A better solution to this problem would be through the use of RenderMan's "hierarchical graphics state". Basically we can remember where we were and go back to it later. This is done using the commands `TransformBegin` and `TransformEnd`. `TransformBegin` remembers all the transformations that have been declared previously, while `TransformEnd` restores the state back to what it was at the previous `TransformBegin`.

```
TransformBegin
        Translate -1 0 0
        Sphere 1 -1 1 360
TransformEnd
```

draws a sphere offset to the left, but leaves things exactly as they were before we started. If we now translate right and draw a sphere it will appear on the right rather than just back in the middle as shown in Figure 7.3 and Listing 7.3.

Listing 7.3 Grouping transforms.

```
#beginend.rib
Display "beginend.tiff" "file" "rgb"
Projection "perspective"
WorldBegin
    #move everything back 2 units
    Translate 0 0 2

    TransformBegin
        #Everything that follows is one unit left
        Translate -1 0 0
        Sphere 1 -1 1 360
    TransformEnd

    TransformBegin
        #Everything that follows is one unit right
        Translate 1 0 0
        Sphere 1 -1 1 360
    TransformEnd
WorldEnd
```

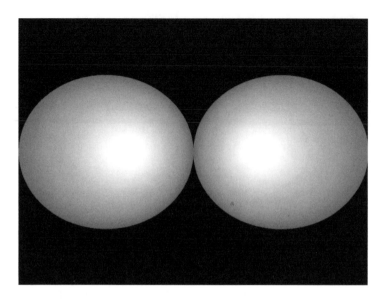

Figure 7.3 Grouping transforms.

Using hierarchical transforms

While this may seem a convoluted method of defining transforms, it allows parts of the RIB to be grouped into logical blocks that reflect how elements of the scene are connected together. This becomes more important when we use more complex transformations.

For example, let us suppose you decide to use spheres to create a cartoon character. The character's head can basically be defined as a sphere. To this we need to add two ears – also spheres – as in Figure 7.4. Listing 7.4 shows how one ear is translated left, while the other is translated right. They are then positioned on top of his head by a single translate applied to both.

Listing 7.4 A head with ears.

```
#ears.rib
Display "ears.tiff" "file" "rgb"
Projection "perspective"
```

```
WorldBegin
    #move everything back
    Translate 0 0 3

    #Head
    Sphere 1 -1 1 360

    TransformBegin
        #Ears
        Translate 0 1.3 0
        TransformBegin
            #Left Ear
            Translate -0.75 0 0
            Scale 0.5 0.5 0.5
            Sphere 1 -1 1 360
        TransformEnd

        TransformBegin
            #Right Ear
            Translate 0.75 0 0
            Scale 0.5 0.5 0.5
            Sphere 1 -1 1 360
        TransformEnd
    TransformEnd
WorldEnd
```

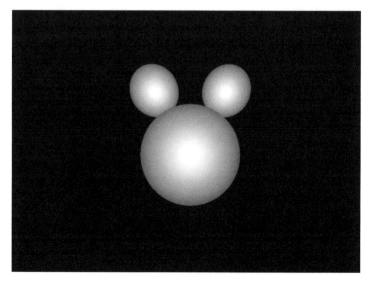

Figure 7.4 A head with ears.

We've made the ears from spheres, but scaled them to make them smaller. The command for scaling is Scale and it takes three parameters allowing objects to be scaled by varying amounts in the x, y and z directions. While the ears are scaled equally in all directions, if we want to create a nose then we want it to be elongated away from the head. This corresponds to the z axis, and hence we make the third parameter of Scale slightly larger, as in Listing 7.5. Note that we don't have to worry about the translations we've applied to the ears, as these are within transform blocks. The TransformBegin and TransformEnd commands allow us to position the nose relative to the head, rather than the ears.

To make this stretching of the nose more obvious in Figure 7.5, we've rotated the whole head. Rotation is specified by an angle through which to rotate, and a line to rotate about. We want to rotate the head 45 degrees about the vertical (y) axis, so we specify a vector of 0,1,0.

Listing 7.5 A scaled nose.

```
#head.rib
Display "head.tiff" "file" "rgb"
Projection "perspective"
WorldBegin
    #move everything back
    Translate 0 0 3

    Rotate 45 0 1 0

    #Head
    Sphere 1 -1 1 360

    TransformBegin
        #Ears
        Translate 0 1.3 0
        TransformBegin
            #Left Ear
            Translate -0.75 0 0
            Scale 0.5 0.5 0.5
            Sphere 1 -1 1 360
        TransformEnd

        TransformBegin
```

```
            #Right Ear
            Translate 0.75 0 0
            Scale 0.5 0.5 0.5
            Sphere 1 -1 1 360
        TransformEnd
    TransformEnd

    TransformBegin
        #Nose
        Translate 0 0 -1.1
        Scale 0.3 0.3 0.5
        Sphere 1 -1 1 360
    TransformEnd

WorldEnd
```

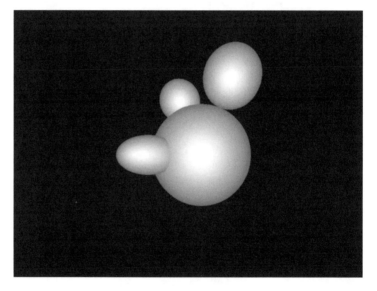

Figure 7.5 A scaled nose.

Though the mechanism of specifying transformations seems strange, it allows groups of commands to be treated as blocks. The nose is currently modelled by a scaled sphere, but it could be replaced by something more complex, which itself contained transforms, without affecting the rest of the RIB. The nose block draws the nose relative to the head. We can then position the head relative to the body, as in Listing 7.6. We can do this without worrying about the ears or the nose, as they always follow the head. When we rotate the head, the nose and ears move with it, as seen in Figure 7.6.

Listing 7.6 Putting the head on a body.

```
#body.rib
Display "body.tiff" "file" "rgb"
Projection "perspective"
WorldBegin
    #move everything back and down
    Translate 0 0 3
    Translate 0 -1 0

    TransformBegin
        Translate 0 1.5 0
        Scale 0.5 0.5 0.5
        Rotate -30 0 1 0

        #Head
        Sphere 1 -1 1 360

        TransformBegin
            #Ears
            Translate 0 1.3 0
            TransformBegin
                #Left Ear
                Translate -0.75 0 0
                Scale 0.5 0.5 0.5
                Sphere 1 -1 1 360
            TransformEnd

            TransformBegin
                #Right Ear
                Translate 0.75 0 0
                Scale 0.5 0.5 0.5
                Sphere 1 -1 1 360
            TransformEnd
        TransformEnd

        TransformBegin
            #Nose
            Translate 0 0 -1.1
            Scale 0.3 0.3 0.5
            Sphere 1 -1 1 360
```

```
         TransformEnd
    TransformEnd

    #Body
    Sphere 1 -1 1 360
WorldEnd
```

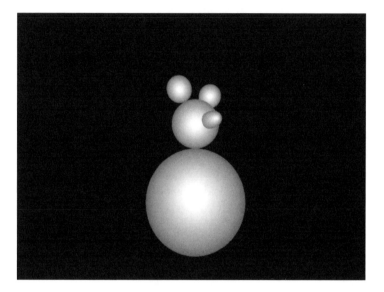

Figure 7.6 Putting the head on a body.

A simple rule to remember is that transforms are applied from the centre outwards, so the nose is specified, and then scaled and positioned in relation to the head. The head itself is positioned relative to the body, which is positioned relative to the camera.

Suggested activities

Using spheres as markers, experiment with using transforms to position objects. Pay particular attention to the order in which different types of transform are applied. Practise grouping transforms together until you can predict the results of a render before viewing the results.

Summary

```
Translate x y z
Scale x y z
Rotate angle x y z
TransformBegin
TransformEnd
```

Related commands

Identity

This command resets the current transformation back to the way it was at WorldBegin.

Transform a b c d e f g h i j k l m n o p

ConcatTransform a b c d e f g h i j k l m n o p

These allow transformations to be specified as a 4 × 4 homogeneous matrix. This format is more complex than the simple commands, but allows any combination of scales, rotates, translations and other transformations to be specified by a single command. An introduction to homogeneous coordinate systems can be found in most computer graphics books.

Chapter

8

Simple Surfaces

Introduction

RenderMan supports a broad range of surface types, capable of reproducing virtually any shape. However, the more general surfaces can be difficult to use when you're constructing RIB files by hand. In many cases, interesting scenes can be constructed from simple geometric shapes such as spheres, cones and cylinders which can be rendered with the minimum of effort. In this chapter we'll examine some RenderMan commands to render these kinds of objects in more detail.

Spheres

We've already used the Sphere command in many of our scenes, allowing us to set up basic renders, and experiment with transformations. So far, however, we've avoided examining the command itself in any detail. If you consider that Sphere takes four parameters it should become apparent that it is capable of more flexibility than might first be thought.

The first parameter of Sphere specifies the radius – that is, the size of the sphere. While this is geometrically identical to a scaled sphere of fixed radius, the resulting image can be different when shading is taken into account. For now you can simply choose whichever method of sizing your sphere is most convenient. To position the sphere you must use Translate, as spheres are always created at the origin.

The second and third parameters of the Sphere command allow you to clip the bottom and top of the sphere, creating a ring. For example the command Sphere 2 -0.5 1 360 would draw a sphere of radius two with most of the bottom removed, and a little of the top clipped, as shown in Listing 8.1 and Figure 8.1. Top and bottom are with respect to the z axis, which normally points into the screen, so to obtain a useful view of this we need to rotate the sphere such that z is aligned vertically.

Listing 8.1 Clipping a sphere.

```
#clipped.rib
Display "clipped.tiff" "tiff" "rgb"
Projection "perspective"
WorldBegin
    Rotate -90 1 0 0
    Translate 0 -4 0
    Sphere 2 -0.5 1 360
WorldEnd
```

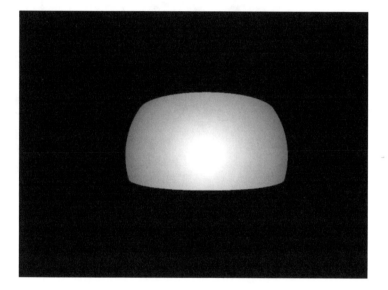

Figure 8.1 *Clipping a sphere.*

The final parameter of the Sphere command is the sweep angle. Rather than drawing the full 360 degrees of the sphere you can choose to draw only part of it, rather like a slice of a pie. In Listing 8.2 we've specified a sweep angle of 270 degrees, so Figure 8.2 shows only three-quarters of a full sphere. Note that this sweep is about the z axis.

Listing 8.2 The sweep angle of a sphere.

```
#sweep.rib
Display "sweep.tiff" "file" "rgb"
Projection "perspective"
```

```
WorldBegin
    Translate 0 0 4
    Sphere 2 -2 2 270
WorldEnd
```

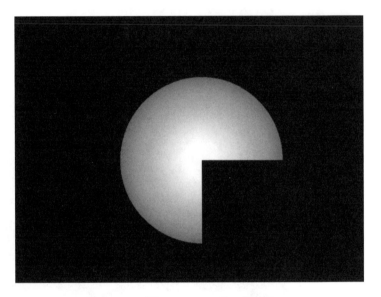

Figure 8.2 *The sweep angle of a sphere.*

While Sphere is a somewhat limited modelling primitive, it demonstrates a number of important issues about the RenderMan API. The Sphere command describes what we want to be drawn, not how it should be drawn. In other rendering APIs such as OpenGL or Mental Ray you might have to pass a number of triangles or rectangles describing the sphere, or at least specify the level of detail with which it should be drawn. This leads to problems when you want to re-render a scene at a higher resolution, or use an extreme zoom on a simple model. The level of detail you have manually assigned for one image may not be appropriate in another.

While RenderMan does have commands to control the quality of the final image, the geometry we have passed to it is defined in a high level format. It is up to the renderer to decide how a sphere can best be rendered, and from the simple description it should be able to produce an image which appears perfectly smooth regardless of scale. While some renderers may choose to break the sphere into polygons, others may prefer to deal with the sphere as a single object. Regardless of how the renderer chooses to deal with geometry, this kind of implementation detail should always be hidden from us.

Though not particularly flexible, Sphere and the other the primitives introduced in this chapter are very efficient to render and simple to texture, as will be seen in Part 3. They also represent a perfectly smooth surface in an incredibly compact form, reducing RIB creation time and saving disk space. You should therefore use these simple surfaces in preference to more complex geometry whenever possible.

Cones and cylinders

In addition to spheres you can create other simple geometric surfaces including cones and cylinders. Like spheres, these are always created at the origin and oriented about the z axis, then transformed to the required location. In addition they all take a sweep angle, allowing only part of the object to be drawn.

To draw a cone you need to specify the radius of the base, and the height. For example `Cone 2 0.5 360` draws a cone of height 2, and a base radius of 0.5. The cone is positioned so that the origin is at the centre of the base.

A cylinder requires a height and a radius. However, rather than specifying a height above the base, as in the case of a cone, a cylinder extends both up and down the z axis, and hence you must specify two distances. `Cylinder 0.5 -1 1 360` draws a cylinder two units high (–1 to 1 along the z axis) and 1 unit in diameter (twice the radius of 0.5). These quadratic surfaces are shown in Figure 8.3, and the equivalent RIB is in Listing 8.3.

Listing 8.3 A cone and cylinder.

```
#coneCyl.rib
Display "coneCyl.tiff" "file" "rgb"

WorldBegin
Rotate -90 1 0 0
Translate 0 -8 0

TransformBegin
    Translate -3 0 -2
    Cone 5 2 360
TransformEnd

TransformBegin
    Translate 3 0 0
    Cylinder 2 -3 3 360
TransformEnd

WorldEnd
```

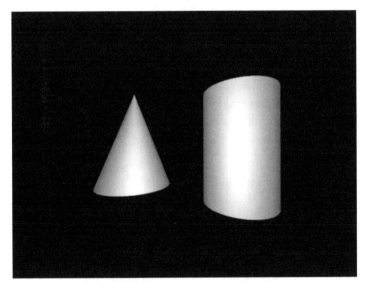

Figure 8.3 A cone and cylinder.

The parameters to Cylinder and Cone are summarized in Figure 8.4.

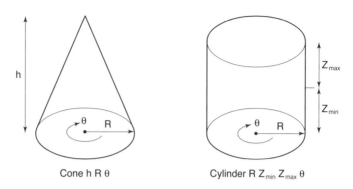

Cone h R θ   Cylinder R Z_{min} Z_{max} θ

Figure 8.4 *The cone and cylinder commands.*

Tori

The Torus command is slightly more complex as it draws a doughnut. This requires two radii – one known as the major radius from the centre of hole in the torus to the centre of the actual "dough", and the second minor radius defining the thickness of the "dough". These are followed by two sets of sweep angles as shown in Figure 8.5. The minor sweep is specified first. It has the additional control of having a start and end angle.

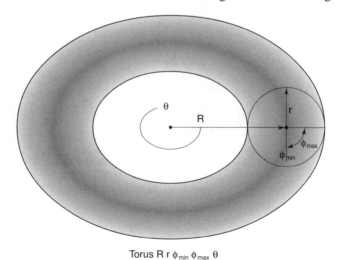

Torus R r ϕ_{min} ϕ_{max} θ

Figure 8.5 *The Torus command.*

Suggested activities

Using only these simple primitives it is possible to construct relatively complex scenes as seen in Figures 8.6 (also Plate V) and 8.7 (also Plate IV). Once correctly shaded and textured even the simplest geometry can produce visually interesting images. The bottom right image on Plate I uses one sphere, three cylinders, and a number of flat planes, yet appears more complex through the use of shading, which you'll learn about in Part 3.

Try to observe real world objects in terms of these basic primitives. Use transformations and the simple geometric surfaces introduced in this chapter to construct an aesthetically interesting composition.

Figure 8.6 *A robot created using only simple surfaces (also Plate V).*

Figure 8.7 *John the Bear (also Plate IV).*

Summary

```
Sphere radius zmin zmax sweep
Cylinder radius zmin zmax sweep
Cone height radius sweep
Torus majrad minrad phimin phimax sweep
```

Related commands

Disk height radius sweep

This command draws a disk around the z axis of the specified radius. Unlike the other simple surfaces the disk can be moved up and down using the height parameter. This is useful for capping the end of cylinders which are otherwise open.

Paraboloid rmax zmin zmax sweep
Hyperboloid x1 y1 z1 x2 y2 z2 sweep

These commands draw two more complex geometric surfaces – the paraboloid and hyperboloid. A paraboloid is simply the 3D equivalent of the 2D parabola produced by the equation $y = x^2$ as shown in Figure 8.8. A hyperboloid is formed by rotating a line about the z axis. This can be used to produce disks, cones, cylinders, lamp shades and other more interesting shapes, as shown in Figure 8.9.

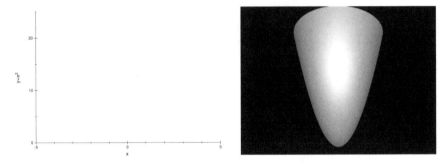

Figure 8.8 *The parabola and paraboloid.*

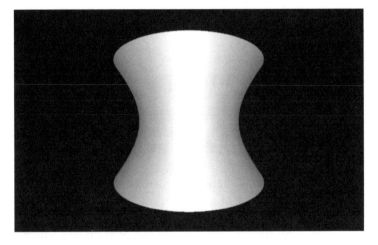

Figure 8.9 *The hyperboloid.*

Chapter 9

Colour and other Attributes of Objects

Introduction

In addition to the geometry itself, we often need to specify properties of an object such as its colour, which affect its appearance. In this section you will be introduced to the most common attributes, and learn how they can be managed.

Colour

The objects we've drawn so far have all been white. However, we can easily specify that an object should be drawn in some other colour by using the Color command. Though RenderMan supports more complex forms of colour control, in practically all cases this is followed by three values enclosed in square brackets, specifying the amount of red, green and blue required in the object. For example, if you wanted to make an object red you simply need to add the command: Color [1 0 0]. Like transforms, colours apply to everything that follows them, so the code in Listing 9.1 produces two red spheres (Figure 9.1). Of course this colour is only a starting point for determining the colour the object will appear in the rendered scene, as lighting and other shading effects must be taken into account. The final colour will be determined by a shader, but in most cases Color is a good approximation to the final result.

Colour is just one special case of an attribute. Attributes are properties of objects which modify the way they are drawn.

Listing 9.1 Using Color.

```
#red.rib
Display "red.tiff" "file" "rgb"
Projection "perspective"

WorldBegin
    Translate 0 0 2

    Color [ 1 0 0 ]
```

```
      TransformBegin
          Translate -1 0 0
          Sphere 1 -1 1 360
      TransformEnd

      TransformBegin
          Translate 1 0 0
          Sphere 1 -1 1 360
      TransformEnd
WorldEnd
```

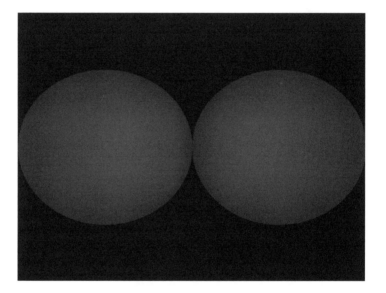

Figure 9.1 Using colour.

Grouping attributes

In the same way that you use TransformBegin/End to manage the scope of transforms, a similar pair of commands: AttributeBegin and AttributeEnd save and restore the current attributes. Using AttributeBegin/End allows us to draw an object, and be certain that it will have no effect on any other objects, as shown in Listing 9.2. This selects red as the current colour, and then enters an Attribute block. Even though the colour is changed to yellow in order to draw the left-hand sphere, the previous colour (red) is restored upon exit from the Attribute block, so the right sphere appears red in Figure 9.2.

Transformations are a special case of attributes, so AttributeBegin performs the action of TransformBegin implicitly, and similarly for AttributeEnd.

Listing 9.2 Controlling the scope of attributes.

```
#beginend.rib
Display "beginend.tiff" "file" "rgb"
Projection "perspective"

WorldBegin
    Translate 0 0 2

    Color [ 1 0 0 ]

    AttributeBegin
        Translate -1 0 0
        Color [ 1 1 0 ]
        Sphere 1 -1 1 360
    AttributeEnd
    #This resets the colour back to red

    AttributeBegin
        Translate 1 0 0
        Sphere 1 -1 1 360
    AttributeEnd

WorldEnd
```

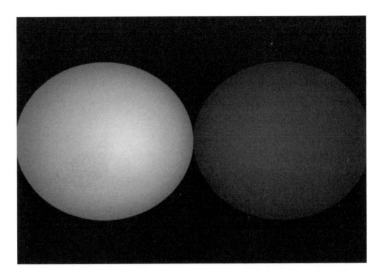

Figure 9.2 Controlling the scope of attributes.

Opacity

A second important attribute is opacity. In the same way that the `Color` command allows you to specify how light is reflected from the surface, you can use `Opacity` to specify how light is transmitted though the surface. When light is shone at a surface from the front, the light reflected back depends on the colour of the light and the colour of the surface. When a light is shone through a surface from behind, then the colour of the light seen through the surface depends on the colour of the light and the opacity of the surface. Opacity is therefore also specified as a colour. For example, in Listing 9.3 we've asked the renderer to draw two spheres, which overlap each other. The green sphere has a transparency of [0.5 0.5 0.5] – that is, it lets half of the light through, regardless of its colour – and hence you can see the red sphere inside the green one in Figure 9.3.

The opacity of a surface can potentially be very different to its colour. For example, stained glass is highly coloured when viewer in transmitted light (opacity), yet appears very dull or even black when viewed in reflected light (colour). You might set the colour and opacity of some red glass to [0.1 0.1 0.1] and [1 0 0] respectively.

Listing 9.3 Opacity.

```
#Opacity.rib
Display "opacity.tiff" "file" "rgb"
Projection "perspective"

WorldBegin
    Translate 0 0 2

    Color [ 1 0 0 ]

    AttributeBegin
        Translate -0.25 0 0
        Color [ 0 1 0 ]
        Opacity [ 0.5 0.5 0.5 ]
        Sphere 1 -1 1 360
    AttributeEnd

    AttributeBegin
        Translate 0.25 0 0
        Sphere 1 -1 1 360
    AttributeEnd
WorldEnd
```

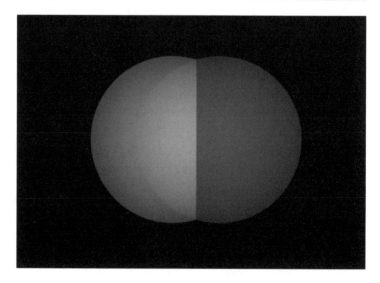

Figure 9.3 Opacity.

Other attributes

ShadingRate

Calculation of the final colour is performed at multiple points on the surface of each object. The number of points required for each object is automatically calculated by the renderer, but under certain circumstances you might want to modify the default value. This is controlled through the command ShadingRate. The default shading rate of 1.0 should be adequate in most cases, but a higher value (ShadingRate 5.0) allows you to trade quality for reduced render times. A lower value (ShadingRate 0.4) may help you to remove certain kinds of artifacts caused by the renderer not using enough points. The effect of increasing shading rate is shown in Listing 9.4 and Figure 9.4 – note how the shading becomes less smooth and more blocky as the shading rate is increased from left to right.

Listing 9.4 Changing the shading rate.

```
#shading.rib
Display "shading.tiff" "file" "rgb"

WorldBegin
    Translate 0 0 6

    ShadingRate 1
    Translate -1.5 0 0
    Sphere 0.5 -0.5 0.5 360

    ShadingRate 2
    Translate 1 0 0
    Sphere 0.5 -0.5 0.5 360

    ShadingRate 4
    Translate 1 0 0
    Sphere 0.5 -0.5 0.5 360
```

```
    ShadingRate 8
    Translate 1 0 0
    Sphere 0.5 -0.5 0.5 360
WorldEnd
```

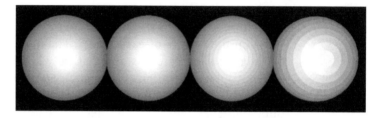

Figure 9.4 *Changing the shading rate.*

Matte

When computer graphics are combined live action, a proxy object is sometimes placed in the CG scene to represent a real world object which will later be composited into place. This object should not appear in the final render, but will still obscure objects behind it. Such an object is known as a matte, and hence this property is specified by the Matte attribute. Matte 1 indicates that the object should be treated in this special way, while Matte 0 specifies a regularly rendered object. To make practical use of the Matte attribute you need to tell the renderer to generate an alpha channel, by setting the final parameter of Display to be "rgba".

Shaders

The shaders applied to an object to describe its surface characteristics are also attributes but these are of sufficient complexity and importance that they deserve a chapter in their own right.

Suggested activities

Add basic colours to the scene you produced for the previous chapter. Plate IV shows a coloured version of our teddy bear.

Try adding a semitransparent object to your scene. Experiment with different colours of opacity as well as simply setting each component to the same.

Experiment with ShadingRate to speed up your test renders.

Summary

```
AttributeBegin
AttributeEnd
Color [ r g b ]
Opacity [ r g b ]
Matte bool
ShadingRate size
```

Related commands

Sides n
Orientation "handedness"
ReverseOrientation

When you render an object it usually has a front and back, but provided the object is opaque, from any single point of view you can only see the front. Even though it seems obvious, you can't see the back of objects, the renderer may have to do a lot of work to figure that out for itself. You may be able to reduce render time dramatically by giving the renderer a hint that it only need draw half the object. If the

Sides attribute is set to 1 then the renderer will immediately throw away the back of objects.

For various reasons the renderer may inadvertently throw away the wrong side – removing the front rather than the back. You can control this by passing "inside" or "outside" to the Orientation command. ReverseOrientation tells it to draw the other side to the one it would normally draw.

Attribute "attributeType" "name" [val]

Though Pixar included many possible attributes in RenderMan standard, they also included a mechanism for developers of renderers to add their own using the Attribute command. These are typically arranged in groups, sharing a common first parameter, and then a more specific attribute name as the second. The value of the parameter follows, in square brackets. Refer to your renderer's documentation to find out what attributes it supports.

Chapter 10

Camera Set-Up

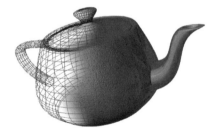

Introduction

A renderer is much like a camera in that it turns a three-dimensional scene into a two-dimensional image. Just as a real camera has many controls that affect exactly how the image should be recorded, so the renderer can record the same scene in a range of different ways. In this section we will examine some of the options available for controlling the final image.

Options

Attributes control parameters that are specified on a per-object basis. In addition to these, some parameters apply to the whole image. These could be considered as defining the virtual camera that is being used to view the scene, and are known as "options". As options apply to the whole scene, they cannot be changed while a frame is being rendered. You can't place `Option` commands between the `WorldBegin` and `WorldEnd` commands. We've already used the `Display` and `Projection` options to control where the rendered image is to be stored, and how three-dimensional space is to be reduced down to two dimensions.

Field of view

You may have noticed that many of the images produced so far appear distorted at the edges. This is an artifact of the projection being used, and the large field of view. By default an image rendered using the perspective projection is rendered with a 90-degree field of view, corresponding to a very wide-angle lens (Listing 10.1 and Figure 10.1). You can reduce this distortion by moving the objects further away from the camera and then reducing the field of view to simulate zooming in with a telephoto lens as shown in Figure 10.2. Field of view is specified by passing a "`fov`" parameter to the perspective projection, as in Listing 10.2.

Listing 10.1 Field of view = 90.

```
#fovnear.rib
Display "fovnear.tiff" "file" "rgb"
Projection "perspective" "fov" [ 90 ]

WorldBegin
    Translate 0 0 2

    TransformBegin
        Translate -1 0 0
        Sphere 1 -1 1 360
    TransformEnd

    TransformBegin
        Translate 1 0 0
        Sphere 1 -1 1 360
    TransformEnd
WorldEnd
```

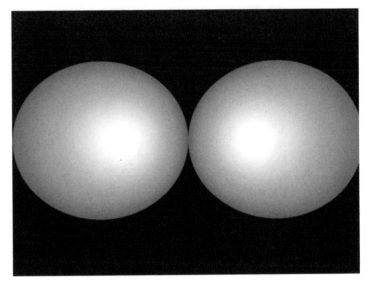

Figure 10.1 Field of view = 90.

Listing 10.2 Field of view = 20.

```
#fovfar.rib
Display "fovfar.tiff" "file" "rgb"
Projection "perspective" "fov" [ 20 ]

WorldBegin
    Translate 0 0 10

    TransformBegin
        Translate -1 0 0
        Sphere 1 -1 1 360
    TransformEnd

    TransformBegin
        Translate 1 0 0
        Sphere 1 -1 1 360
    TransformEnd
WorldEnd
```

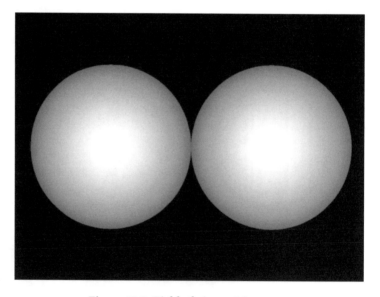

Figure 10.2 *Field of view = 20.*

In the following chapters we'll use this mechanism of passing parameters by specifying their name followed by one or more values enclosed in square brackets with many commands.

Positioning the camera

As the camera is the only fixed point of reference in our scene, it can't be moved as such but we can produce the same effect by moving all of the objects in the world. We've done this previously by placing transforms within the WorldBegin/End block. However, by placing transforms after the Projection command and before the WorldBegin command you can explicitly transform the whole world. The position of the world is specified in terms of the camera, objects are specified in terms of the world, and hence this effectively moves the camera.

At present it will have no effect upon your images whether you place transforms inside or outside of the world block, and merely serves as a useful convention to distinguish camera movement from object movement. However, the ability to distinguish the position of an object relative to a static world even when the camera is moving will become more important when we start to shade our objects in Part 3.

This is demonstrated in Listing 10.3.

Listing 10.3 Setting options.

```
#exposure.rib
Display "exposure.tiff" "file" "rgb"
Format 640 480 1.0
Clipping 5 15
PixelSamples 2 2
Exposure 1.0 2.2

Projection "perspective" "fov" [ 25 ]

Translate 0 0 10

WorldBegin
    Sphere 2 -2 2 360
WorldEnd
```

Clipping

When a scene is rendered, the renderer will try and discard any objects which are too close or too far away from the camera. Those too far away are redundant because they simply won't be visible, while objects close to the camera are difficult to render, and probably off screen anyway. However, the renderer needs some hints as to what should be considered too close or too far away. You can give the renderer this information using the Clipping command and its two parameters, hither and yon.

Any parts of an object closer than hither will be removed, as will those beyond yon. Hither in particular is worth paying attention to if any geometry is close to the camera, as by increasing hither only slightly you can dramatically improve render times. When correctly set this option should not affect the rendered image.

The Clipping command is used in Listing 10.3, where the sphere is positioned 10 units back. Anything closer than 5 or further than 15 units would be discarded.

Image resolution

We've so far been rendering our images at 640 pixels wide by 480 pixels high, as this is the default output resolution. However, you can control the resolution of the final image by using the Format command. This takes a height and width for the output image measured in pixels. A third parameter specifies the pixel aspect ratio.

Most computer displays have square pixels – an image 100 $\times$ 100 pixels would appear square in screen, but this is not the case for many video formats which tend to squash the image slightly. If your image is to be displayed on such a device then you need to make sure this squash is taken into account during rendering by setting the pixel aspect ratio appropriately. A frame for output on PAL video might therefore contain the line `Format 768 576 0.9`. More immediately you might want to reduce the size of the output image in order to speed up test renders using `Format 320 240 1.0`.

Super sampling

Though `Format` specifies how many pixels the render needs to output, internally it will calculate the colour at many more points for each output pixel, averaging them together to produce the final pixel colour. This "super sampling" reduces rendering artifacts, and produces a higher quality image, at the cost of additional render time. You can control the number of points calculated per pixel by using the `PixelSamples` command. A setting of `PixelSamples 1 1` will render quickly using only one sample per pixel, while a setting of `PixelSamples 4 4` will evaluate 16 samples per pixel. Depending upon the renderer, these sixteen samples will be roughly arranged in a 4 × 4 grid.

Exactly how many samples you need to use depends on the contents of your image, and what you intend to use it for. Consider Figure 10.3 which consists of three images rendered with increasing samples. The first image is clearly blocky at the edges of the sphere, while the second is a distinct improvement. The third image is marginally better but for this simple image the effect is not particularly marked. When we start experimenting with advanced techniques such as depth of field and motion blur you will probably need to increase PixelSamples to avoid artifacts.

Listing 10.3 explicitly sets the output resolution and super sampling to their default values of 640 × 480, and 2 × 2.

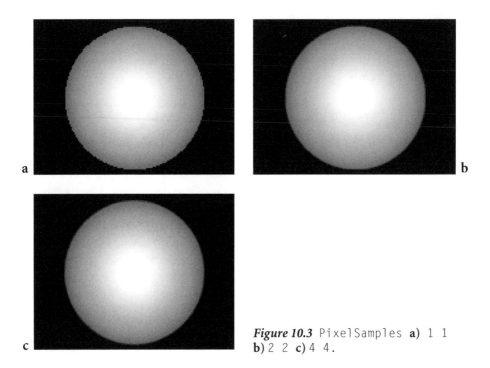

Figure 10.3 PixelSamples **a)** 1 1 **b)** 2 2 **c)** 4 4 .

Exposure

Having finally calculated the correct colour of each pixel, we need to display the resultant image. Unfortunately such things are rarely simple. The value calculated by the renderer is "linear" – that is, a pixel with a brightness of 0.8 should appear twice as bright as a pixel with a brightness of 0.4. While you probably consider this a perfectly normal situation, it is not the result that is obtained when an image is sent to a typical video device. Most devices have a non-linear response, which would result in the 0.4 pixel being much darker than it should be. This non-linearity is known as gamma, and can be summarized for individual devices, or more generally for a type of device by a single number. A gamma value of one would represent a linear device, while most computer screens have a value in the range 1.5 to 2.0.

Some official standards for video screens specify a gamma value of 2.2, but this is not particularly reliable.

When previewing images it is important that you use imaging software which corrects the gamma of the image being displayed to match the display on which it is being viewed. However, when you're rendering the final results, which will then be transferred to a specific output device such as video tape, a higher quality image can be produced by gamma correcting in the renderer. You can do this by using the `Exposure` command (Listing 10.3), which takes two parameters – `gain` and `gamma`. `Gain` is simply a multiplier which makes the image brighter or darker. `Gamma` generates a non-linear image. Figure 10.4 is rendered with a gamma of 2.2, resulting in the edges of the sphere which have previously been very dark, appearing much lighter.

Figure 10.4 Increasing gamma.

If your output device requires a gamma correction of 2.2 then including the command `Exposure 1.0 2.2` will produce an image with a better balance between the light and dark areas *when viewed on the target output device.* Viewing on a linear device would make it appear washed out. You should only use this approach when the image generated is being sent directly to the output device, as any compositing or colour correction that may be done post-render cannot be applied to non-linear images. In such cases it would be more appropriate to output linear images, which can be gamma corrected after they have been processed.

Suggested activities

Use the new options you have learnt to set up the camera in your scene in a fashion that is both practical and aesthetically pleasing.

Adjust parameters like `PixelSamples`, and `Resolution` to render in a timely fashion

Experiment with gamma correction and exposure to produce images which appear consistently good both on your monitor, and on any output devices which may be available to you.

Summary

```
Projection "projectionname" "fov" [ angle ]
Clipping hither yon
Format xres yres pixelaspect
PixelSamples x y
Exposure gain gamma
```

Related commands

PixelFilter "filtername" xwidth ywidth

While it may appear counter-intuitive, simply adding together all the samples generated for a pixel does not produce the best possible final image. For reasons that are somewhat complex, a higher quality image can be produced by weighting the samples such that samples near the centre of the pixels are considered more important. Samples from outside the pixel may also be included, some samples even being subtracted rather than added. The method used to calculate the average pixel colour is controlled by the `PixelFilter` command.

Quantize scale min max dither

By default most renderers will produce an eight bits per channel image, with black being stored as zero, and white being stored as 255. The `Quantize` command allows images to be stored at a higher level of detail such as 16 bit or floating point format, and gives some control over how brightness levels are represented.

Option "OptionType" "name" [val]

Just as the `Attribute` command allows renderers to define new properties of objects, so the `Option` command allows additional camera controls not originally included in the RenderMan API to be specified.

Chapter

11

Lighting

Introduction

A well-constructed scene consists of more than just objects and a camera. The positioning and control of lighting is an essential aspect, whether you're attempting to create a realistic, theatrical or cinematic atmosphere. In this chapter we will look at the various types of light that are available in RenderMan renderers, and see how you can use these in a RIB file. These will allow you to illuminate your scene in a more interesting fashion than the default lighting we have so far been using.

A plastic object

All the objects we have created so far have had a simple lighting model applied to them – surfaces which are square on to the camera are bright, while those at an acute angle appear darker. This default model gives an adequate sense of depth and has allowed us to create basic scenes, but for greater realism we need surfaces which can reflect light in more interesting ways.

One of the most powerful features of a RenderMan renderer is the support for shaders. These allow the appearance of an object to be controlled in almost any fashion imaginable. We'll consider shaders in the following chapter, but more immediately we need something which can be lit by the lights we're about to create. The shader "plastic", which produces the standard computer-generated look, is perfect for this. You simply need to include the line Surface "plastic" in the RIB file and any objects that follow will be made out of plastic. Shaders are applied on a per object basis, and hence are attributes. As such they are stored and recalled by AttributeBegin and AttributeEnd.

Upon attaching the plastic shader and rendering the scene you should be rewarded with a totally black image. The default surface is self-illuminating, but most shaders including plastic require some kind of lighting – as in real life without any lights, a plastic object will simply appear black.

Pointlight

You can create a light by using the LightSource command. Like surfaces, lights are controlled by shaders, but several standard lights are available. The "pointlight" shader creates a light that shines equally in all directions, rather like a naked light bulb. By default it is centred at the origin, so we can move it around using the standard transform commands. It is usually more convenient, however, to place the light using a "from" parameter, as in Listing 11.1.

Listing 11.1 Pointlight.

```
#pointlight.rib
Display "pointlight.tiff" "file" "rgb"
Projection "perspective" "fov" [ 30 ]

Translate 0 0 5

WorldBegin
    LightSource "pointlight" 1
        "from" [ -2 2 -2 ]
        "intensity" [ 7 ]

    Surface "plastic"
    Color [ 1 0 0 ]
    Sphere 1 -1 1 360
WorldEnd
```

Parameter lists of this kind can be applied to many commands – we used them previously to specify the field of view of the camera – and take the form of a parameter name followed by an array of values enclosed in square brackets. Fortunately, parameters always have default values so we can ignore any parameters that we aren't interested in.

For a "pointlight" the only other parameter you will regularly need to modify is "intensity". When first placed in a scene the pointlight source often appears dim because it is defined to obey an inverse square law – for each doubling of distance from the light the intensity drops by a factor of four. This is exactly how lights behave in the real world, but many other renderers use a different lighting model, as non-physically based lights can make it easier to light scenes in an aesthetically pleasing (though less realistic) fashion. It is very simple to define a new kind of light in RenderMan, but for now you need simply note that intensity will probably have a value greater than one, as it will be attenuated over the distance from light to surface.

The result of illuminating a red plastic sphere with a point light source is shown in Figure 11.1 (also Plate I).

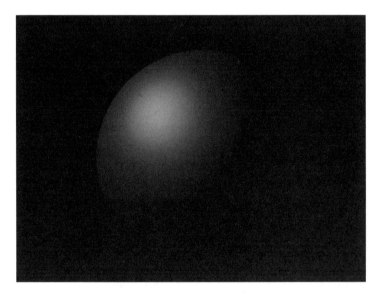

Figure 11.1 *Pointlight (also Plate I).*

The number following the shader name is a light source handle – simply a unique number by which you can refer to the light later in the RIB file. This allows you to create lights at the beginning of a scene, and then apply them only to certain objects, giving greater control. The Illuminate command is used to turn lights on and off, and takes two parameters: a light handle followed by 1 for on or 0 for off. This is shown in Listing 11.2 where two light sources and two spheres are created. Illuminate is used to turn off light source 1 for the second sphere. Close examination of Figure 11.2 shows that while the left-hand sphere has two highlights, the right only has one.

The state of a light source is an attribute, and hence it is possible to save and restore the currently active lights using AttributeBegin/End.

Listing 11.2 Turning a light off and on.

```
#illuminate.rib
Display "illuminate.tiff" "file" "rgb"
Projection "perspective" "fov" [20]
Translate 0 0 10

WorldBegin
    LightSource
        "pointlight" 1
        "from" [4 3 -5]
        "intensity" [16]
    LightSource
        "pointlight" 2
        "from" [-4 3 -5]
        "intensity" [16]

    Surface "plastic"
    Color [ 1 0 0 ]

    AttributeBegin
        Illuminate 1 1
        Translate -0.5 0 0
        Sphere 1 -1 1 360
    AttributeEnd

    AttributeBegin
        Illuminate 1 0
        Translate 0.5 0 0
        Sphere 1 -1 1 360
    AttributeEnd
WorldEnd
```

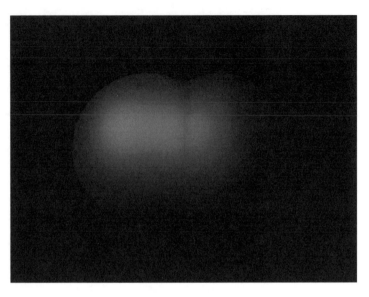

Figure 11.2 Turning a light off and on.

Distantlights

While the point light has a position, but no orientation, certain light sources have an orientation, but effectively no position. These are known as "distantlights" and are typically used to represent daylight. The illumination of an object lit by the sun changes little as the object moves within the scene (excluding shadows). However, illumination is highly dependent on the object's orientation – is it facing towards the sun or away from it?

To create a "distantlight" you therefore need to specify a "to" parameter that describes the direction in which the light is shining. Listing 11.3 creates a light shining to the right, the results of which can be seen in Figure 11.3 (also Plate I).

Listing 11.3 Distantlight.

```
#distantlight.rib
Display "distantlight.tiff" "file" "rgb"
Projection "perspective" "fov" [ 30 ]
```

```
Translate 0 0 5

WorldBegin
    LightSource "distantlight" 1
        "to" [ 1 0 0 ]
        "intensity" [ 1 ]

    Color [ 1 0 0 ]
    Surface "plastic"
    Sphere 1 -1 1 360
WorldEnd
```

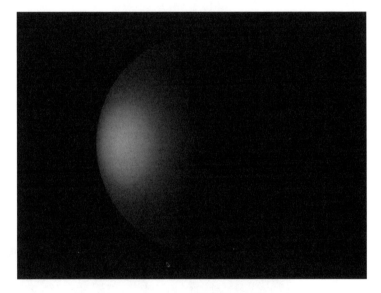

Figure 11.3 *Distantlight (also Plate I).*

Spotlights

Just as in cinema or theatre, when maximum control over the lighting of scene is required, you should use some form of spotlight. The standard "spotlight" shader provided with all RenderMan implementations behaves like a standard theatrical spotlight and hence has both a position and an orientation, specified using a "from" and a "to" parameter.

However, whereas the "to" of a distantlight specifies a direction, the "to" of a spotlight specifies a point towards which the spot is pointing. In Listing 11.4 we've created a spotlight, illuminating a plastic sphere. By specifying "to" as [0 0 0] the spotlight points towards the centre of the sphere. A spotlight produces a circular beam as shown in Figure 11.4 (also Plate I).

Listing 11.4 Spotlight.

```
#spotlight.rib
Display "spotlight.tiff" "file" "rgb"
Projection "perspective" "fov" [ 30 ]

Translate 0 0 5

WorldBegin
    LightSource "spotlight" 2
        "from" [-2 2 -2]
        "to" [ 0 0 0 ]
        "intensity" [ 7 ]
        "coneangle" [0.25]
        "conedeltaangle" [0.05]

    Color [ 1 0 0 ]
    Surface "plastic"
    Sphere 1 -1 1 360
WorldEnd
```

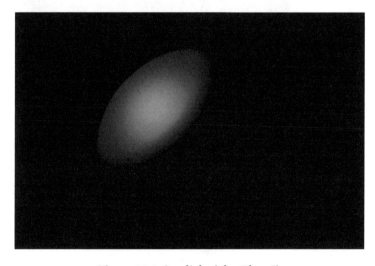

Figure 11.4 Spotlight (also Plate I).

A spotlight also allows you to control exactly how directional the light is using the "coneangle" and "deltaangle" parameters, illustrated in Figure 11.5. Outside of "coneangle" (specified in radians) the light has no effect, while within coneangle-deltaangle the full intensity of the light is in effect. Between these two angles the light falls off smoothly producing a soft edge to the beam. This can be seen in Figure 11.6 where the delta angle (specified in Listing 11.5) has been increased to produce a softer edge to the light.

Listing 11.5 Softening the edge of a spot.

```
#delta.rib
Display "delta.tiff" "file" "rgb"
Projection "perspective" "fov" [ 30 ]

Translate 0 0 5

WorldBegin
    LightSource "spotlight" 2
        "from" [-2 2 -2]
        "to" [ 0 0 0 ]
        "intensity" [ 7 ]
        "coneangle" [0.25]
        "conedeltaangle" [0.25]

    Color [ 1 0 0 ]
    Surface "plastic"
    Sphere 1 -1 1 360
WorldEnd
```

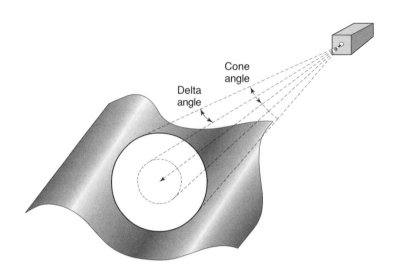

Figure 11.5 *Cone angle and delta angle.*

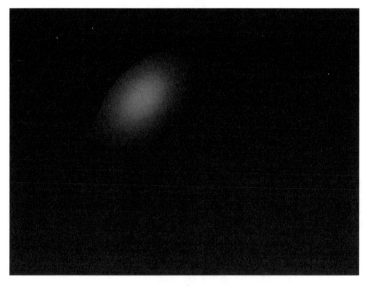

Figure 11.6 *Softening the edge of a spot.*

Ambient lights

In the real world each light source would emit light into the scene which would then bounce from surfaces, and illuminate other surfaces which are not directly lit. In computer graphics this is known as global illumination and is modelled using techniques such as radiosity and photon mapping. All methods of global illumination are incredibly slow, however, and therefore impractical for many applications. In such cases you can fake this indirect illumination by simply adding a little extra light to each surface using an "ambientlight" source.

We've defined an ambient light in Listing 11.6, which illuminates all surfaces equally regardless of their position or orientation. A consequence of this is that it removes clues as to the depth of the scene, as can be seen in the resultant image in Figure 11.7. If you use it in combination with other lights, however, adding as little as possible to avoid areas of total black, it can soften your lighting and produce a better image. Listing 11.7 combines an ambient light with a spotlight to produce the image in Figure 11.8 (also Plate I).

Listing 11.6 Ambient light.

```
#ambientlight.rib
Display "ambientlight.tiff" "file" "rgb"
Projection "perspective" "fov" [ 30 ]

Translate 0 0 5

WorldBegin
    LightSource "ambientlight" 1
                "intensity" [ 0.5 ]

    Color [ 1 0 0 ]
    Surface "plastic"
    Sphere 1 -1 1 360
WorldEnd
```

Figure 11.7 Ambient light.

Listing 11.7 Ambient and spotlight.

```
#spotambient.rib
Display "spotambient.tiff" "file" "rgb"
Projection "perspective" "fov" [ 30 ]

Translate 0 0 5

WorldBegin
    LightSource "ambientlight" 1
                "intensity" [ 0.1]
    LightSource "spotlight" 2
                "from" [-2 2 -2]
                "to" [ 0 0 0 ]
                "intensity" [ 7 ]
                "coneangle" [0.25]
                "conedeltaangle" [0.05]


    Color [ 1 0 0 ]
    Surface "plastic"
    Sphere 1 -1 1 360
WorldEnd
```

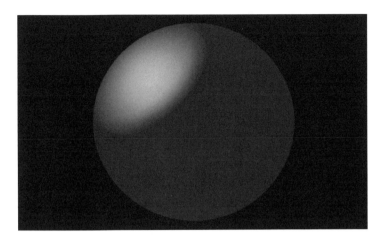

Figure 11.8 *Ambient and spotlight (also Plate I).*

Suggested activities

Change your scene so that all the objects are made of plastic. Add a small amount of ambient light so you can still see the objects, then place light sources of various types into the scene to illuminate it in a pleasing fashion. Figure 11.9 (also Plate V) shows the results lighting the bear scene.

Figure 11.9 *John the Bear with lighting.*

Many renderers support other lights in addition to the standard ones. Uberlight, for example, provides a much greater degree of control than any of the standard lights, including options for avoiding many of the inconveniences of physics. Investigate any other light source types that may be provided with your renderer.

Summary

```
Surface "shadername" ...
LightSource "shadername" handle ...
Illuminate handle bool
LightSource "pointlight" 1
   "from" [ x y z ]
   "intensity" [ val ]
   "color" [ r g b ]
LightSource "distantlight" 2
   "to" [ x y z ]
   "intensity" [ val ]
   "color" [ r g b ]
LightSource "spotlight" 3
   "from" [ x y z ]
   "to" [ x y z ]
   "intensity" [ val ]
   "color" [ r g b ]
   "coneangle" [ angle ]
   "conedeltaangle" [angle]
LightSource "ambientlight" 4
   "intensity" [ val ]
   "color" [ r g b ]
```

Chapter 12

The Standard Shaders

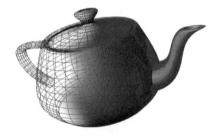

Introduction

Having set up some lights, we can now consider how those lights interact with the surfaces in our scene. This interaction is controlled by a surface shader. Shaders are one of the most important aspects of RenderMan, to such an extent that the second half of this book will be totally dedicated to shader writing. However, before we consider how you can write your own shaders we'll first examine the standard shaders that are defined by the RenderMan standard and are available by default in all renderers.

Constant

The simplest surface is "constant". Even simpler than the default surface we've used previously, the constant shader simply takes the colour defined in the RIB and uses it as the output colour, ignoring all lighting in the scene. Naturally this results in a totally flat appearance, as in Figure 12.1, and is of limited use when generating photo-realistic images. You might choose to use it, however, to produce images that are deliberately stylized.

Figure 12.1 The "constant" shader.

Listing 12.1 shows the basic RIB file used to look at shaders in this chapter. A spotlight is used to provide the key light of the scene, while an ambient is used to fill in the dark side. The shader – in this case "constant" – is attached to a sphere using the command Surface.

Listing 12.1 The "constant" shader.

```
#constant.rib
Display "constant.tiff" "file" "rgb"
Projection "perspective" "fov" [ 30 ]

Translate 0 0 5

WorldBegin
    LightSource "ambientlight" 1
                "intensity" [ 0.1]
    LightSource "spotlight" 2
                "from" [-2 2 -2]
                "to" [ 0 0 0 ]
                "intensity" [ 7 ]
                "coneangle" [0.25]
                "conedeltaangle" [0.05]

    Color [ 1 0 0 ]
    Surface "constant"
    Sphere 1 -1 1 360
WorldEnd
```

Matte

For most applications we require something which takes into account the lighting of the scene, and the position of the surface to give the appearance of depth. This can be achieved using the surface shader "matte", as shown in Figure 12.2 (also Plate II). This simulates the diffuse scattering of light from a rough surface (such as a brown envelope). When light in the scene hits a matte object it is scattered in all directions. As a result the colour of the surface as it appears when rendered is independent of where you place the camera.

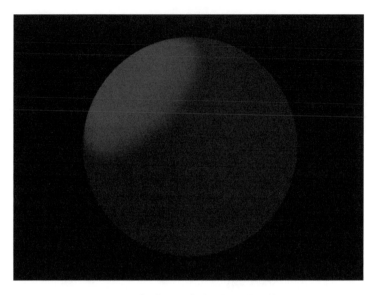

Figure 12.2 The "matte" shader (also Plate II).

As with most of the other surface shaders, "matte" also responds to ambient light that has no direction. The amount of ambient and diffuse light scattered by the matte surface can be scaled using the parameters "Ka" and "Kd" respectively.

The matte shader should not be confused with the Matte command. The two are totally unrelated and the unfortunate clash of names is purely coincidental.

Metal

Metallic objects are usually identifiable by the way they reflect bright light, creating a sharp specular highlight. In contrast to the matte shader, the location of this bright spot on the surface is highly dependent on the position of the observer. Light hitting a metallic surface is reflected as if in a mirror, and only when viewed from near the mirror angle will the highlight be visible.

Of course not all metal surfaces are as highly polished, and in these cases, the light will be scattered in a cone around the mirror angle, the size of which depends on the roughness of the surface – a rough surface will produce a less sharply defined highlight, while a smooth surface would produce a small and sharp bright point.

You can simulate these effects by use of the "metal" shader which is illustrated in Figure 12.3 (also Plate II). The brightness of the highlight can be controlled by the "Ks" parameter, while the size of the highlight is set by the "roughness" parameter.

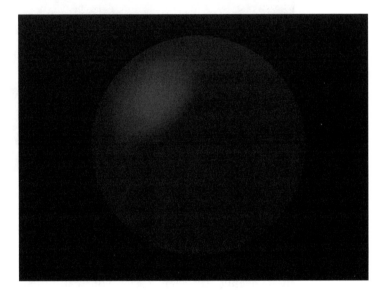

Figure 12.3 The "metal" shader (also Plate II).

Plastic

By examining a plastic surface, you should be able to observe that such materials generally combine both a diffuse and a specular component. Coloured plastic is manufactured by suspending particles of colour inside a clear "glue". Light can either be reflected in a specular fashion from the smooth surface of the glue producing a white highlight, or scattered randomly from the coloured particles like a matte surface. The "plastic" shader shown in Figure 12.4 (also Plate II) therefore has all of the parameters of both "matte" and "metal". In addition it allows the colour of the specular highlight to be controlled by the parameter "specularcolor".

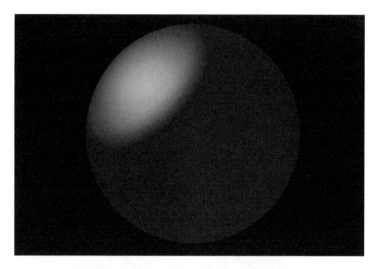

Figure 12.4 The "plastic" shader (also Plate II).

When you wish to create a metal surface, it is likely that you'll find the standard metal shader difficult to control. Its lack of a diffuse component results in surfaces that are difficult to light evenly. In such cases you can create a metallic appearance using the plastic shader by setting specularcolor to be the same as the standard RIB colour. By setting Ks to 1 and Kd to 0, the results will be identical to the metal shader, but by increasing Kd (and reducing Ks if necessary), you can fill in the dark areas of the surface without relying too heavily on ambient light.

Painted plastic

The most complex standard shader, "paintedplastic", extends plastic by allowing a texture map to be used to control the base colour, rather than the uniform RIB colour. The name of the image file is passed to the shader using the parameter "texturename", as in Listing 12.2. If you were to apply the texture file shown in Figure 12.5, the resultant image would be Figure 12.6 (also Plate II).

Listing 12.2 The "paintedplastic" shader.

```
#painted.rib
Display "painted.tiff" "file" "rgb"
Projection "perspective" "fov" [ 30 ]

Translate 0 0 5

WorldBegin
    LightSource "ambientlight" 1
              "intensity" [ 0.1]
    LightSource "spotlight" 2
              "from" [-2 2 -2]
              "to" [ 0 0 0 ]
              "intensity" [ 7 ]
              "coneangle" [0.25]
              "conedeltaangle" [0.05]

    Color [ 1 0 0 ]
    Surface "paintedplastic" "texturename" ["swirl.tiff"]
    Rotate 90 1 0 0
    Sphere 1 -1 1 360
WorldEnd
```

Figure 12.5 *A sample texture file.*

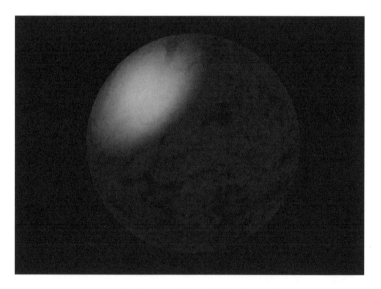

Figure 12.6 *The "paintedplastic" shader (also Plate II).*

The format of the image file is dependent upon the renderer, and while many renderers will accept the TIFF file format, in most cases you can increase rendering speeds by using a format specific to the renderer. These formats are optimized for texture lookup, and can dramatically reduce memory requirements when rendering large images with large textures. For PRMan the command to generate these optimized image files is txmake – running the command "txmake image.tiff image.tx" creates "image.tx". BMRT uses the command mkmip in the same fashion to create a special format of TIFF file that can also be used efficiently.

Suggested activities

While the shaders covered here are required to be supported by all RenderMan compliant renderers, your renderer may have been supplied with a number of additional shaders. Check the release notes, and investigate using any other shaders that you may have available. Use these along with the standard shaders to make your scene more interesting. Figure 12.7 (also Plate V) shows the robot scene rendered with appropriate lighting and shading. Make good use of the Ka, Kd, Ks and specularcolor parameters where available. Despite the metallic appearance, many of the surfaces in the robot image are plastic, with appropriate parameter settings.

Figure 12.7 *The robot scene with lighting and shading (also Plate V).*

Investigate the texture file formats that your renderer supports, and the commands required to generate these. How are the textures wrapped onto the surfaces?

Summary

```
Surface    "constant"
Surface    "matte"  "Ka" [ 1]
           "Kd" [ 1 ]
Surface    "metal"  "Ka" [ 1]
           "Ks" [ 1 ]
           "roughness" [0.1]
Surface    "plastic"
           "Ka" [ 1 ]
           "Kd" [ 0.5 ]
           "Ks" [ 0.5 ]
           "roughness" [ 0.1 ]
           "specularcolor" [ 1 1 1 ]
Surface    "paintedplastic"
           "Ka" [ 1]
           "Kd" [ 0.5 ]
           "Ks" [ 0.5 ]
           "roughness" [0.1]
           "specularcolor" [ 1 1 1 ]
           "texturename" [ "" ]
```

Related commands

Displacement "name" ...

Surface shaders are used to control the surface colour of an object but RenderMan supports many other types of shaders that you can use to control other aspects of the rendering process. One shader of each type may be attached to an object.

A displacement shader, specified with the Displacement command (Listing 12.3) allows you to deform a surface, adding creases, bumps, scratches or other fine details which would be difficult to produce using geometry. Such a shader is demonstrated in Figure 12.8. Note that the displacement shader is specified in addition to a surface shader – the surface is still made of plastic even though it has been displaced. Though there are no standard displacement shaders, many renderers ship with a number of displacement shaders such as "dented".

Listing 12.3 A displacement shader.

```
#dented.rib
Display "dented.tiff" "file" "rgb"
Projection "perspective" "fov" [ 30 ]

Translate 0 0 5

WorldBegin
    LightSource "ambientlight" 1
                "intensity" [ 0.1]
    LightSource "spotlight" 2
                "from" [-2 2 -2]
                "to" [ 0 0 0 ]
                "intensity" [ 7 ]
                "coneangle" [0.25]
                "conedeltaangle" [0.05]

    Color [ 1 0 0 ]
    Surface "plastic"
    Displacement "dented"
    Sphere 1 -1 1 360
WorldEnd
```

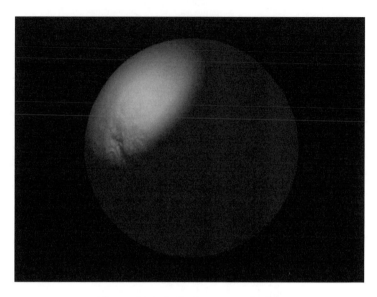

Figure 12.8 A displacement shader.

Chapter

13

More
Complex
Surfaces

Introduction

While objects like spheres and cones have allowed us to create elegant geometry from a small number of simple commands, we clearly need more flexible surfaces that will allow us to model a wider range of shapes. In this chapter we will introduce a number of surface types that allow you to create almost any form of object.

Polygons

Though it has a number of limitations, the easiest method of constructing a surface is to approximate it using a number of flat polygons. This allows you to produce any shape to any required level of detail. In fact many non-RenderMan renderers use polygons as their only form of geometry.

Simple polygons

You can generate polygons in RenderMan by using the Polygon command, which draws a single polygon. The corners of this polygon are specified as points in counter-clockwise order by a parameter "P". For example, the command shown in Listing 13.1 draws a unit square in the *xy* plane, as can be seen in Figure 13.1. This polygon has four corners, but any number may be used provided that they are co-planer – that is, the polygon must be flat.

Listing 13.1 A simple polygon.

```
#polygon.rib
Display "polygon.tiff" "file" "rgb"
Projection "perspective" "fov" [ 30 ]

Translate -0.5 -0.5 3
```

```
WorldBegin
    LightSource "ambientlight" 1
                "intensity" [ 0.1 ]
    LightSource "pointlight" 2
                "from" [ -2 2 -2 ]
                "intensity" [ 7 ]

    Color [ 1 0 0 ]
    Surface "plastic"
    Polygon "P" [ 0 0 0
                  1 0 0
                  1 1 0
                  0 1 0]
WorldEnd
```

Figure 13.1 *A simple polygon.*

General polygons

The Polygon command also has the restriction that the polygon must be convex: if you were to draw a line from any point in the polygon to any other point in the polygon, that line is not allowed to cross any of the edges of the polygon. To render concave polygons you must use the command GeneralPolygon. This is slightly more complex to use, as it also allows you to cut holes into the polygon. Despite the relaxing of other restrictions general polygons must still be planer.

A general polygon is made from one or more "loops", each of which may contain any number of points. The first loop defines the boundary of the polygon, while subsequent loops cut holes into it. To define a GeneralPolygon you must first tell the renderer how many points comprise each loop, and then provide an array of points containing all of the points, for each loop in turn. For example, in Listing 13.2 the GeneralPolygon command is followed by an array with two elements 4 and 3 indicating that the polygon to be drawn is a quadrilateral (actually a square) with a triangle cut out from it. The first four points of the "P" parameter define the square, and the next three define the triangle, as shown in Figure 13.2.

Listing 13.2 A general polygon.

```
#general.rib
Display "general.tiff" "file" "rgb"
Projection "perspective" "fov" [ 30 ]

Translate -0.5 -0.5 3

WorldBegin
    LightSource "ambientlight" 1
                "intensity" [ 0.1 ]
    LightSource "pointlight" 2
                "from" [ -2 2 -2 ]
                "intensity" [ 7 ]

    Color [ 1 0 0 ]
    Surface "plastic"
    GeneralPolygon [4 3]
        "P" [ 0 0 0
              1 0 0
              1 1 0
              0 1 0
```

```
                    0.1 0.1 0
                    0.9 0.1 0
                    0.5 0.9 0]
WorldEnd
```

Figure 13.2 A general polygon.

"Curved" polygons

When you connect polygons together to create a more complex model, there is invariably a crease where two parts meet, as seen in the top half of Figure 13.3. While this is an accurate representation of the geometry we've passed to the renderer, this crease is undesirable if we're using polygons to approximate a curved surface. The problem is that while the two surfaces are joined together without a gap, there is still a sharp change in the orientation of the surface which results in an obvious change in the shaded colour. To make things worse, our eyes are particularly tuned to pick out these kinds of edges.

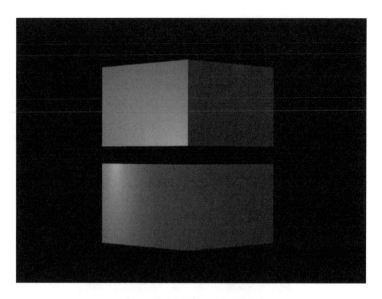

Figure 13.3 Phong shading.

You can reduce this artifact, and create a smoother appearance by interpolating normals across the surface – a technique known as Phong shading. While the surfaces are still flat, the orientation of points on the surface are faked so the points on coincident edges are not only in the same place but are shaded to have the same colour. To achieve this effect in RenderMan you must explicitly assign normals to the vertices of the polygon using the "N" parameter. The polygons in the bottom half of Figure 13.3 are identical to those in the top half, but Listing 13.3 reveals that surface normals have been added so that points on the edge where the two polygons meet are shaded similarly on both sides of the join.

Listing 13.3 Phong shading.

```
#phong.rib
Display "phong.tiff" "file" "rgb"
Projection "perspective" "fov" [ 30 ]

Translate -0.5 -0.5 3

WorldBegin
```

```
LightSource "ambientlight" 1
            "intensity" [ 0.1 ]
LightSource "pointlight" 2
            "from" [ -2 0.5 -2 ]
            "intensity" [ 7 ]

Color [ 1 0 0 ]
Surface "plastic"

# "Flat" Polygons, have a crease when joined
Polygon "P" [   0.0 0.55  0.0
                0.5 0.55 -0.25
                0.5 1.0  -0.25
                0.0 1.0   0.0]
Polygon "P" [   0.5 0.55 -0.25
                1.0 0.55  0.0
                1.0 1.0   0.0
                0.5 1.0  -0.25]

#Normals Assigned to hide join`
Polygon "P" [   0.0 0.0   0.0
                0.5 0.0  -0.25
                0.5 0.45 -0.25
                0.0 0.45  0.0]
        "N" [   0.25 0 0.5
                0.00 0 1.0
                0.00 0 1.0
                0.25 0 0.5 ]
Polygon "P" [   0.5 0.0  -0.25
                1.0 0.0   0.0
                1.0 0.45  0.0
                0.5 0.45 -0.25]
        "N" [   0.00 0 1.0
               -0.25 0 0.5
               -0.25 0 0.5
                0.00 0 1.0 ]
WorldEnd
```

The surface is shaded as if it were a smooth curve from one side to the other. Closer examination of the profile of the object reveals, however, that it is still in fact comprised of two flat polygons. Phong shading is a useful trick that can help to hide the limitation of polygonal models but if your intention is to create a smoothly curving surface then the results will always be an approximation.

Patches

Despite their flexibility, the use of polygons is discouraged when RenderMan is used. Though many simple renderers handle polygons well, they do not fit comfortably into the complex shading pipeline that high quality rendering requires. You should only use polygons for objects consisting of large flat surfaces, rather than using many tiny polygons to approximate curves surfaces. RenderMan provides commands to create curved surfaces directly and wherever possible you should use these in preference.

The starting point for these curved surfaces is the humble `Patch` command. Before considering curved patches, however, we must look at flat patches, which are technically known as bilinear. A bilinear patch is simply a polygon with four corners and while this limitation makes it more difficult to model with, there are pay-offs at the shading stage. Listing 13.4 demonstrates the creation of a patch, and generates a square identical to the polygon shown in Figure 13.1.

Listing 13.4 A patch.

```
#patch.rib
Display "patch.tiff" "file" "rgb"
Projection "perspective" "fov" [ 30 ]

Translate -0.5 -0.5 3

WorldBegin
    LightSource "ambientlight" 1
                "intensity" [ 0.1 ]
    LightSource "pointlight" 2
                "from" [ -2 2 -2 ]
                "intensity" [ 7 ]

    Color [ 1 0 0 ]
    Surface "plastic"
    Patch "bilinear"
            "P" [ 0 0 0
                  1 0 0
```

```
                        0 1 0
                        1 1 0]
WorldEnd
```

Though the `Patch` command may appear very similar to the `Polygon` command it should be noted that a bilinear patch always takes 4 points in the "P" array, and the order of the vertices has changed, as patches are specified a row at a time, rather than around the boundary. The different ordering of points is illustrated in Figure 13.4. Unlike polygons, patches need not be planer, and hence the patch in Listing 13.5 where we've twisted the top two points around is perfectly valid and can be seen in Figure 13.5, while an equivalent polygon may not be guaranteed to render correctly.

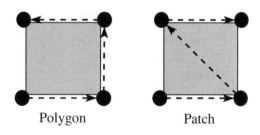

Polygon   Patch

Figure 13.4 Ordering of points.

Listing 13.5 A curved "linear" patch.

```
#curved.rib
Display "curved.tiff" "file" "rgb"
Projection "perspective" "fov" [ 20 ]

Translate -0.5 -0.5 4

WorldBegin
    LightSource "ambientlight" 1
                "intensity" [ 0.1]
    LightSource "pointlight" 2
                "from" [-2 2 -2]
                "intensity" [ 7 ]

    Color [ 1 0 0 ]
```

```
      Surface "plastic"
      Patch "bilinear" "P" [   0 0 0
                               1 0 0
                               0.4 1 1    #MOVED BACK
                               0.6 1 -1]  #MOVED FORWARDS
WorldEnd
```

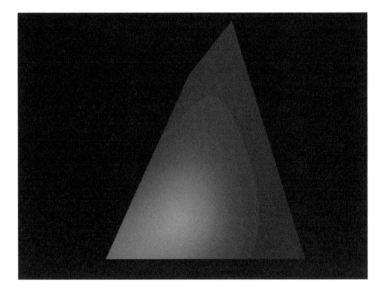

Figure 13.5 A curved "linear" patch.

Cubic patches

If you took nine bilinear patches and arranged them into a grid as in Figure 13.6a you could approximate a curved surface by moving those points around to form something like Figure 13.6b. However, the surface would look even better if instead of joining the points together using flat patches we could somehow fit curves through the points as in Figure 13.6c.

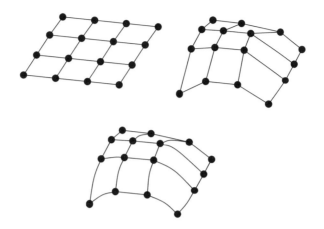

Figure 13.6 Joining patches: (a) a group of linear patches; (b) approximating a curve; (c) interpolating the points.

This is exactly what happens when we use a bicubic patch. We need 16 points, which are specified a row at a time, as shown in Figure 13.7, to create the necessary faceted surface, which is known as a control hull, and then the renderer simply fits a perfectly smooth curved surface to that hull.

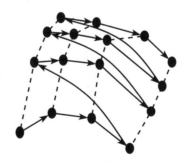

Figure 13.7 Control points in a cubic patch.

We've created a bicubic patch in Listing 13.6. While it is somewhat hard to interpret, the points around the edge of the grid have been placed in a square, while the points in the centre have been displaced up and down to create an interesting surface, as seen in Figure 13.8.

Listing 13.6 A bicubic patch.

```
#cubic.rib
Display "cubic.tiff" "file" "rgb"
Projection "perspective" "fov" [ 30 ]

Translate -0.5 -0.5 3

WorldBegin
  LightSource "ambientlight" 1
            "intensity" [ 0.1 ]
  LightSource "pointlight" 2
            "from" [ -2 2 -2 ]
            "intensity" [ 10 ]

  Color [ 1 0 0 ]
  Surface "plastic"
  Rotate 40 1 0 0

  Patch "bicubic" "P" [0 0    0 0.4 0    0 0.6 0    0 1 0    0
                       0 0.4 0 0.4 0.4 3 0.6 0.4 -3 1 0.4 0
                       0 0.6 0 0.4 0.6 -3 0.6 0.6 3 1 0.6 0
                       0 1    0 0.4 1    0 0.6 1    0 1 1    0]
WorldEnd
```

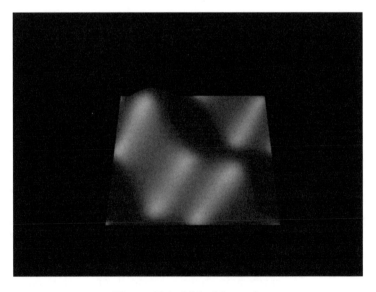

Figure 13.8 A bicubic patch.

Suggested activities

Add any flat surfaces required by your scene using polygons or bilinear patches as appropriate. We can finally give the bear something to sit on, as shown in Figure 13.9 (also Plate V).

Experiment with bicubic patches to introduce a few more interesting shapes.

Figure 13.9 John the Bear with flat surfaces and shading added
(also Plate IV).

Summary

```
Polygon ...
GeneralPolygon [ nverts per loop ] ...
Patch "type" ...
```

Related commands

PointsPolygons [nverts per loop] [loop verts] ...
PointsGeneralPolygons [loops per poly] [nverts per loop] [loop verts] ...

When polygons are used to model a surface, you inevitably have many polygons with corners and edges in common with their neighbours. Rather than passing such a surface to the renderer through a large number of separate Polygon commands, you can combine many polygons together in a single command using the PointsPolygons and PointsGeneralPolygons commands. By exploiting the shared vertices, the RIB file will be more compact, and the renderer can treat the set of polygons as a single object.

PatchMesh "type" nu uwrap nv vwrap ...

In the same way you can combine polygons using PointsPolygons, patches are often specified in groups using the PatchMesh command. PatchMesh creates a mesh of points nu by nv square. This is particularly useful for bicubic patches, as it ensures that individual patches join together smoothly. By setting uwrap and vwrap to be "periodic" or "nonperiodic" you indicate if the edges of the mesh should be joined together.

Basis ubasis ustep vbasis vstep

When using bicubic patches the renderer must produce a smooth curve based on the control points it has been given. The exact manner in which this is done is controlled by the

Basis command, which allows various standard methods to be selected by name or the user can specify a new form of interpolation using a matrix. It is possible to specify different forms of curve fitting for the rows and columns of the patch.

While some methods produce curves which pass through every point, others use the points as simply a guide. Some methods make it easier to stitch patches together while others give better control over the surface itself.

NuPatch nucv uorder uknot umin umax nvcvs vorder vknnot vmin vmax ... TrimCurve nloops ncurves order know min max n u v w

Though bicubic patch meshes are very versatile there are some forms of curvature which even they can only approximate. Yet more complex surfaces can be described using NURBS (Non-Uniform Rational B-Splines), which are generated by the NuPatch command. Though NURBS patches have much in common with the simpler patches, the parameters to the NuPatch command are probably too complex to construct by hand. Despite this complexity, the greater flexibility afforded makes NURBS surfaces the preferred primitive in most high end modelling packages. RenderMan also allows NURBS to be trimmed using the TrimCurve attribute – holes may be cut into the surface, and edges removed.

Shadows

Introduction

The lights we have used so far have not cast any shadows. While this is acceptable for simple images, shadows are essential if any form of realism is to be established. Shadows tie objects to the surfaces they are resting on, and provide additional visual cues to the relationship of objects in a scene. In this section we will see how shadows are typically created by RenderMan renderers.

Shadow maps

Though certain renderers may support ray traced shadows, the standard method of creating shadows in RenderMan is through the use of shadow maps. This approach is slightly tedious to set up by hand, but it does offer better performance and greater flexibility. Most modelling software can ask RenderMan to generate these maps automatically so there is little additional work for the end user, though the requests to the renderer are considerably more complex than might be expected.

The principle of a shadow map is to create a file that contains information about which points are in shadow with respect to a light placed at a certain point. To create this file the image is simply rendered from the position of the light. Rather than recording the colour of each pixel the renderer records the distance from the camera to the object, as illustrated in Figure 14.1. This is known as a Z buffer. This process is repeated for each light in the scene (or at least all those that are required to cast shadows).

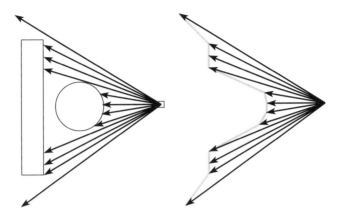

Figure 14.1 How a Z buffer works.

Once a shadow map has been generated for the light, the main render (or beauty pass) can take place. When the renderer needs to determine if a point is in shadow with respect to a particular light, it can consult that light's shadow map. The position of the point in the shadow map is calculated, and if the new point is further away than the distance recorded in the map it is behind something (when viewed from the light), and hence is in shadow.

Generating a shadow map

In practice, we might start with a simple scene consisting of a sphere resting on a linear patch lit by a single spotlight. Such a scene is in Listing 14.1, but as you can see in the rendered image in Figure 14.2, the sphere does not cast a shadow onto the plane.

Listing 14.1 Scene without shadows.

```
#noshadow.rib
Display "noshadow.tiff" "file" "rgb"
Projection "perspective" "fov" [ 30 ]
Clipping 1 10
```

```
Translate 0 0 5

WorldBegin
    LightSource "ambientlight" 1
                "intensity" [ 0.1]
    LightSource "spotlight" 2
                "from" [ 0 4 0 ]
                "to" [ 0 0 0 ]
                "intensity" [ 7 ]
                "coneangle" [0.3]
                "conedeltaangle" [0.05]

    Color [ 1 0 0 ]
    Surface "plastic"
    Sphere 1 -1 1 360

    Color [ 0 1 0 ]
    Patch "bilinear"
        "P" [ -5 -1 -5
               5 -1 -5
              -5 -1  5
               5 -1  5 ]
WorldEnd
```

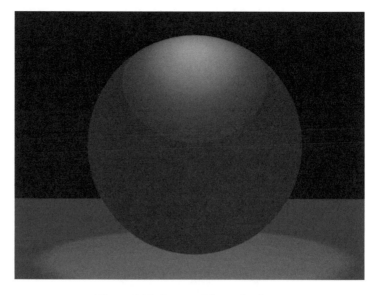

Figure 14.2 *Scene without shadows.*

To add a shadow to the spot the first thing we need to do is render a Z buffer from the position of the light. This is done by placing the camera at the position of the light. When viewed from this position the scene appears as in Figure 14.3.

Figure 14.3 *The scene viewed from the light source.*

Rather than recording the colour of each pixel we modify the Display command, instructing the renderer to record "z", the distances to the visible surfaces as in Listing 14.2. As the light casts a conical beam, we've also changed the Format command to create a square image, capturing all of the points that the light illuminates. The result of this render is an image that is black where there is a surface close to the camera and brighter where objects are further away, as shown in Figure 14.4.

Listing 14.2 Creating the Z buffer image.

```
#makeshadow.rib
Display "zbuffer.tiff" "file" "z"
Format 512 512 1.0
Clipping 1 10

Projection "perspective" "fov" [ 40 ]

Translate 0 0 4
Rotate -90 1 0 0

WorldBegin
    Color [ 1 0 0 ]
    Surface "plastic"
    Sphere 1 -1 1 360

    Color [ 0 1 0 ]
    Patch "bilinear"
            "P" [ -5 -1 -5
                   5 -1 -5
                  -5 -1  5
                   5 -1  5 ]
WorldEnd
MakeShadow "zbuffer.tiff" "map.shad"
```

Figure 14.4 The Z buffer image.

In addition to the depth information, a shadow map also needs to contain information about the camera it was rendered with to enable points to be correctly looked up. This is performed by the MakeShadow command, on the last line of Listing 14.2. This takes a Z buffer that has been rendered and adds the necessary details before writing it to a shadow map file. The field of view of the camera need not be the same as the angle of the light, or indeed the orientation need not be the same, though significant variation would result in wasted time rendering the unused information.

You can use Z buffer images for many purposes besides shadows. By recording the depth of each pixel as well as its colour, effects such as fogging, and depth of field can be added to a scene after it has been rendered. Such an approach is often preferred in a commercial environment, as it allows the depth effect to be changed without re-rendering the scene. A Z buffer also allows you to place new elements into a rendered scene, and have them pass in front of and behind other objects, without having to worry about creating mattes. However, aliasing can be a problem with this technique, and the scene is best rendered at a higher resolution than needed if this approach is taken.

Applying a shadow map

Having created the shadow map we now return to the original version of the scene and replace the "spotlight" with a light of type "shadowspot", as in Listing 14.3. This behaves identically except that it casts shadows based on the map passed in by the parameter "shadowname". Rendering with the new light produces the image found in Figure 14.5.

Listing 14.3 Scene with shadows.

```
#withshadow.rib
Display "withshadow.tiff" "file" "rgb"
Projection "perspective" "fov" [ 30 ]
```

```
Translate 0 0 5

WorldBegin
        LightSource "ambientlight" 1
                    "intensity" [ 0.1]
        LightSource "shadowspot" 2
                    "shadowname" [ "map.shad" ]
                    "from" [ 0 4 0 ]
                    "to" [ 0 0 0 ]
                    "intensity" [ 7 ]
                    "coneangle" [0.3]
                    "conedeltaangle" [0.05]

    Color [ 1 0 0 ]
    Surface "plastic"
    Sphere 1 -1 1 360

    Color [ 0 1 0 ]
    Patch "bilinear"
          "P" [ -5 -1 -5
                 5 -1 -5
                -5 -1  5
                 5 -1  5 ]
WorldEnd
```

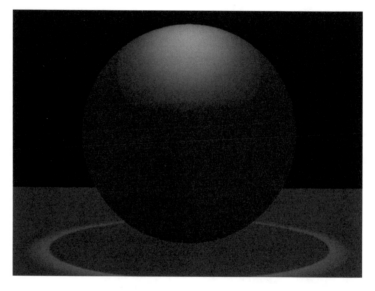

Figure 14.5 *Scene with shadows.*

Note that the shadows are cast by the objects in the map, not in the final render, so if an object is required not to cast a shadow, it should simply not be included in the map. Similarly, in Listing 14.4 we've removed the sphere from the scene, but it is still included in the shadow map. The resultant image in Figure 14.6 therefore contains the shadow of the removed object.

Listing 14.4 Shadow without an object.

```
#nosphere.rib
Display "nosphere.tiff" "file" "rgb"
Projection "perspective" "fov" [ 30 ]

Translate 0 0 5

WorldBegin
    LightSource "ambientlight" 1
               "intensity" [ 0.1]
    LightSource "shadowspot" 2
               "shadowname" [ "map.shad" ]
               "from" [ 0 4 0 ]
               "to" [ 0 0 0 ]
               "intensity" [ 7 ]
               "coneangle" [0.3]
               "conedeltaangle" [0.05]

    Surface "plastic"
    Color [ 0 1 0 ]
    Patch "bilinear"
          "P" [ -5 -1 -5
                 5 -1 -5
                -5 -1  5
                 5 -1  5 ]
WorldEnd
```

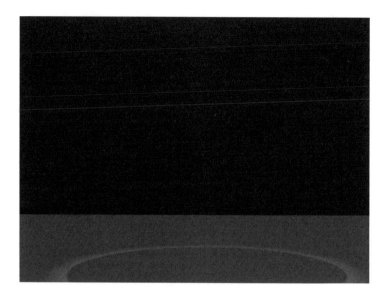

Figure 14.6 *Shadow without an object.*

You can also make point lights cast shadows in a similar fashion using the `shadowpoint` light shader, but six shadow maps are required to cover the faces of a cube enclosing the light. Multiple shadow maps may also be used to handle semi-transparent objects. This approach was used to produce the image in Figure 8.8.

Suggested activities

Pick the most important light in your scene and create a shadow map for it. Replace the light shader you are currently using with an appropriate one that supports shadows, and render the scene with shadows.

Does every light in your scene require a shadow map or are one or two sufficient? Typically a few key shadows should be enough to convince the casual viewer that the lighting is authentic. What happens if you use the shadow map from one light and apply it to a different light?

Summary

```
MakeShadow "zBufferFilename" "ShadowMapFilename"
LightSource "shadowspot" 1
  "from" [ x y z ]
  "to" [ x y z ]
  "intensity" [ val ]
  "color" [ r g b ]
  "coneangle" [ angle ]
  "conedeltaangle" [angle]
  "shadowname" ["Filename"]
```

Related commands

FrameBegin framenumber
FrameEnd

The creation of shadow maps can be done in the same RIB file as the beauty pass by use of FrameBegin and FrameEnd which allow multiple frames to be stored in the same file.

Simply place FrameBegin/End around those commands which relate to each frame.

Display "ShadowMapFilename" "shadow" "z"

The standard method of shadow map creation is to first generate an interim Z buffer file which is then converted to a shadow map by the MakeShadow command. In many implementations of RenderMan, however, you can streamline this two-stage process by specifying an output device of type "shadow". When this is used, the image written to disk automatically gets the appropriate camera information added, and the MakeShadow command is made obsolete.

Chapter
15

Motion Blur and Depth of Field

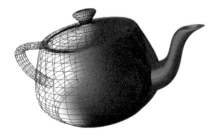

Introduction

Photorealism in computer images is often dependent not on accurately modelling the real world, but in recreating the viewers' expectations of what an image of the real world should look like. Real world images are captured using physical cameras which have limitations and defects, while the simulated digital camera is typically implemented as a perfect pinhole camera. High quality photo-realistic renderers must allow the user to specify a more complex camera model which reintroduces the artifacts that users expect to see in photographs and films.

In this section we will see how the physical limitations of a real camera can be introduced back into the "perfect" virtual camera normally found in computer graphics to produce a more realistic image.

Motion blur

Setting up the shutter

While the simulated camera is perfectly capable of capturing the scene instantly, a real camera needs to expose light onto a film. The camera's shutter must be open for a length of time to allow enough light to enter the lens so that an image can be created. Any objects which move while the shutter is open will appear blurred. Any movement of the camera will result in the blurring of the whole scene.

The length of exposure is a property of the camera and hence applies to the whole scene, making it an option that you must specify prior to the World block. The command to specify this is Shutter, which takes two parameters: the time at which the shutter opens and the time at which the shutter closes. Between these two times the shutter is open and objects will be blurred. The absolute values of these parameters have no effect, but simply provide a reference for defining motion, and therefore can simply be set as Shutter 0.0 1.0 – the shutter opens at time zero and closes at time one.

Note that in a real camera the timing of the shutter would significantly affect the brightness of the image, but here the two effects have been decoupled allowing you to set each to its optimal value. The Exposure command controls brightness while the Shutter command only affects motion blur. Though in a real camera the controls interact in complex ways this only makes operation more difficult, and separating the features like this provides greater flexibility.

Defining motion

When motion blur is in use, most of the scene may still be rendered normally, blur only being applied to those objects which are moving. Objects are positioned by the use of transformations, and hence you can specify that objects are moving by providing a pair of transforms, representing the object's position at the start and end of the shutter period. To indicate that a pair of transformations is a motion rather than simply two consecutive transforms you should enclose them within the commands MotionBegin and MotionEnd.

This is demonstrated in Listing 15.1, which contain a sphere moving 0.4 units along the x axis in the time period 0 to 1. Each motion block can contain exactly one set of transforms, so if an object was both spinning and translating, two consecutive motion blocks would be used, one for the Rotate and one for the Translate.

Listing 15.1 Transformation motion blur.

```
Display "motion.tiff" "file" "rgb"
Projection "perspective" "fov" [ 30 ]
Shutter 0 1
```

```
Translate 0 0 5

WorldBegin
    LightSource "ambientlight" 1
                "intensity" [ 0.1]
    LightSource "spotlight" 2
                "from" [ -2 4 -2 ]
                "to" [ 0 0 0 ]
                "intensity" [ 10 ]
                "coneangle" [0.25]
                "conedeltaangle" [0.05]

    MotionBegin [ 0 1 ]
        Translate 0    0 0
        Translate 0.4 0 0
    MotionEnd
    Color [ 1 0 0 ]
    Surface "plastic"
    Sphere 1 -1 1 360
WorldEnd
```

Depending on the renderer you are using it may be possible to specify more complex motion paths by positioning the object at several locations during the exposure, as shown in Listing 15.2, where the sphere goes up and then back down, as it moves from left to right. The array following MotionBegin contains a list of sample times, and there should be one transformation in the block for each. Separate motion blocks may contain different numbers of samples, at different times, from which the renderer will calculate the resulting motion.

Listing 15.2 A more complex motion path.

```
#path.rib
Display "path.tiff" "file" "rgb"
Projection "perspective" "fov" [ 30 ]
PixelSamples 5 5
Shutter 0 1

Translate 0 0 5

WorldBegin
    LightSource "ambientlight" 1
```

```
                    "intensity" [ 0.1]
     LightSource "pointlight" 2
                    "from" [ -2 4 -2 ]
                    "intensity" [ 10 ]

     MotionBegin [ 0 0.5 1 ]
         Translate -0.5   0    0
         Translate 0.0 0.5 0
         Translate 0.5 0    0
     MotionEnd

     Color [ 1 0 0 ]
     Surface "plastic"
     Sphere 1 -1 1 360
WorldEnd
```

Deformation blur

In addition to the blurring of objects due to transformations, objects may also require blurring because they are changing shape. You can achieve this effect in a similar way to transformation blur by placing several instances of the object inside a motion block. This is demonstrated in Listing 15.3, where a sphere decreases in size, in addition to moving from left to right while the shutter is open.

Listing 15.3 Deformation motion blur.

```
#deform.rib
Display "deform.tiff" "file" "rgb"
Projection "perspective" "fov" [ 30 ]
Shutter 0 1
PixelSamples 3 3

Translate 0 0 5

WorldBegin
    LightSource "ambientlight" 1
                   "intensity" [ 0.1]
    LightSource "spotlight" 2
                   "from" [ -2 4 -2 ]
                   "to" [ 0 0 0 ]
                   "intensity" [ 10 ]
```

```
    Color [ 1 0 0 ]
    Surface "plastic"

    MotionBegin [ 0 1 ]
        Translate -0.5    0 0
        Translate 0.5 0 0
    MotionEnd
    MotionBegin [ 0 1 ]
        Sphere 1.0 -1.0 1.0 360
        Sphere 0.5 -0.5 0.5 360
    MotionEnd
WorldEnd
```

In principle, it should be possible to motion blur any floating point parameter to virtually any command using this approach, though the level of support for motion blur is variable between renderers. Most support the blurring of transformations, though far fewer support deformation. Not all renderers support sample times other than the start and end of the shutter period, and many have problems with non-linear paths such as those generated by motion blurring a rotation.

Depth of field

A similar effect to motion blur is depth of field. Again, it is a deficiency of real world cameras that we are often required to mimic in our computer-generated imagery in order that it meets the cinematic expectations of the audience. Only objects a certain distance from the camera are in focus, and any objects significantly closer or further away will appear blurred. Though it is complex to calculate, depth of field provides important visual cues about the relationship of objects and may also be used for dramatic effect (see plate VII).

Depth of field is specified by the option command DepthOfField which takes three parameters: the f-stop, the focal length and the focal distance. While these parameters are very familiar to traditional photographers, and allow the camera to be matched to live action shots for effects work, they are somewhat confusing when first encountered in a pure computer graphics context.

Focal distance

The simplest parameter is `focaldistance`. This is simply the distance from the camera at which objects will be perfectly in focus, measured in Camera space. By animating this parameter over several frames you can draw the attention of the audience from one object to another.

In order to relate synthetic depth of field to the real world effect we will assume that 1 unit in the RIB file corresponds to 1 m. Listing 15.4 sets up a row of spheres at distances from 1 to 7 m. It also includes a depth of field command. The third parameter of `DepthOfField` specifies the focal distance and this has initially been set to 2. The resulting image in Figure 15.1a shows that the third sphere from the front is in sharp focus while those further back are increasingly blurred. By contrast in Figure 15.1b we've moved the focal distance back to 5 m, resulting in a highly blurred foreground.

a
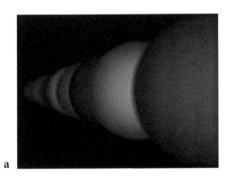
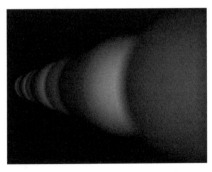
b

Figure 15.1 (a) A close focal distance 2m (`DepthOfField 2.8 0.100 2`); (b) A larger focal distance 5 m (`DepthOfField 2.8 0.100 5`).

Listing 15.4 Depth of field.

```
#near.rib
Display "near.tiff" "file" "rgb"
Projection "perspective" "fov" [ 30 ]

DepthOfField 2.8 0.100 2

Translate 0 0 1

WorldBegin
#1 Meter
    Translate 0.3 0 0
    Color [ 1 0 0 ]
    Sphere 0.25 -0.25 0.25 360

    Translate -0.2 0 0.5
    Color [ 0 1 0 ]
    Sphere 0.25 -0.25 0.25 360

    Translate -0.2 0 0.5
    Color [ 0 0 1 ]
    Sphere 0.25 -0.25 0.25 360

    Translate -0.2 0 0.5
    Color [ 1 0 0 ]
    Sphere 0.25 -0.25 0.25 360

#3 Meters
    Translate -0.2 0 0.5
    Color [ 0 1 0 ]
    Sphere 0.25 -0.25 0.25 360

    Translate -0.2 0 0.5
    Color [ 0 0 1 ]
    Sphere 0.25 -0.25 0.25 360

    Translate -0.2 0 0.5
    Color [ 1 0 0 ]
    Sphere 0.25 -0.25 0.25 360

    Translate -0.2 0 0.5
    Color [ 0 1 0 ]
    Sphere 0.25 -0.25 0.25 360

#5 Meters
    Translate -0.2 0 0.5
```

```
    Color [ 0  0  1 ]
    Sphere 0.25 -0.25 0.25 360

    Translate -0.2 0 0.5
    Color [ 1  0  0 ]
    Sphere 0.25 -0.25 0.25 360

    Translate -0.2 0 0.5
    Color [ 0  1  0 ]
    Sphere 0.25 -0.25 0.25 360

    Translate -0.2 0 0.5
    Color [ 0  0  1 ]
    Sphere 0.25 -0.25 0.25 360
WorldEnd
```

Focal length

The focallength parameter is a property of a particular lens, as it describes the extent to which it bends light. In the real world, a typical wide-angle lens might have a focal length of 35 mm while a telephoto lens could be 200 mm or longer. All things being equal, a longer lens will produce a more blurred image, as only those objects very close to the focal distance are in focus. A shorter lens is more forgiving, and objects stay sharp over a larger range of distances.

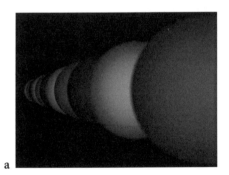
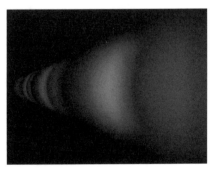

a

b

Figure 15.2 (a) A short focal length 60 mm (DepthOfField 2.8 0.060 4); (b) A long focal length 150 mm (DepthOfField 2.8 0.150 4).

In order to demonstrate this we will use a focal distance of 4 m so the spheres in the centre of the row will be in focus. In Figure 15.2a we've used a 60 mm lens corresponding to a typical medium lens while the image in Figure 15.2b uses a 150 mm lens. As you can see in Figure 15.2a all the spheres except the closest are in sharp focus, while in Figure 15.2b the foreground is extremely out of focus, and some blurring can be seen in the last two spheres.

F-stop

Perhaps the most confusing parameter for the non-photographer is the `f-stop`. However, put most simply: a small `f-stop` will produce a lot of blurring, while a larger `f-stop` will produce less. In a real camera suitable values might be between 1.8 and 22, but this need only be a starting point for experimentation.

In the images used so far, a small `f-stop` of 2.8 has been used to ensure that the effect is noticeable, but in practice a larger value would probably be used. Figure 15.3a uses a 100 mm lens, focused at 4 m with an `f-stop` of 2.8, and produces obvious blurring in the image. However, in the otherwise identical 15.3b we've increased the `f-stop` to 8 and the image is significantly sharper. Taken to the extreme, a very large `f-stop` will remove depth of field effects completely.

In a real camera f-stop is related to the size of the aperture, and hence how much light can enter the camera. Specifying the focal length of the lens also implicitly controls the field of view. However, as was the case for motion blur, these effects are decoupled in the synthetic camera, allowing you to control image brightness and field of view with `Exposure` and `Projection` respectively.

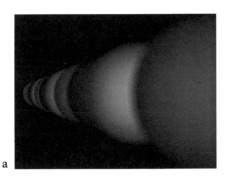 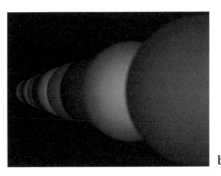

a   b

Figure 15.3 *(a) A larger aperture f/2.8* (`DepthOfField 2.8 0.100 4`);
(b) A small aperture f/8 (`DepthOfField 8 0.100 4`).

Suggested activities

According to the RenderMan standard, both motion blur and depth of field are "optional capabilities" – that is, your renderer may not support them. In practice, virtually all have some support for these features, but it is often limited in some way. Different renderers implement these effects in different ways, and this can result in wide variation in the images produced. This can be particularly obvious when rendering still images rather than animation sequences. Check the release notes to verify exactly what you should expect to work, and then create scenes to test these features.

Add depth of field to your scene, such that the closest and furthest objects are very slightly blurred. If any objects should be moving then use motion blur to increase realism. You may need to increase `PixelSamples` to reduce artifacts when using these effects.

Perhaps the best way to become conformable with concepts such as f-stop and focal length is to borrow a manual focus SLR camera and experiment with the lenses and settings available.

Summary

```
Shutter starttime endtime
MotionBegin [ sampletimes...]
MotionEnd
DepthOfField  f-stop focallength focaldistance
```

Chapter
16

The C API

Introduction

Having established the basic concepts of describing scenes to a renderer using the RIB file format, we can now transfer that knowledge to the more complex, but more powerful C form of the RenderMan interface.

Overview

The RIB file format is an effective way to distribute scenes for rendering, but as a method of generating geometry it can be a little tedious. To create 100 spheres you would need to type 100 `Sphere` commands into the RIB. Specifying large numbers of co-ordinates for patches and polygons by hand is also highly error prone. While viewing and modifying RIB files is a powerful technique of debugging and adapting renders, most RIBs are generated by programs. Even if you're not planning to write your own programs, much of the documentation of RenderMan is written in terms of the C API, and so understanding the nature of the C interface is invaluable.

The C API consists of a set of functions declared in the header file "`ri.h`", which are called by the user's code. Each of these functions corresponds to a single RIB command, and hence adapting between the two interfaces is relatively straightforward. When the program is compiled it is linked with a RIB library so that when the program is run a RIB file is written to disk which can then be rendered in the usual way. This process is shown graphically in Figure 16.1. It may also be possible to link directly to your renderer, in which case running the program will generate the image in a single step.

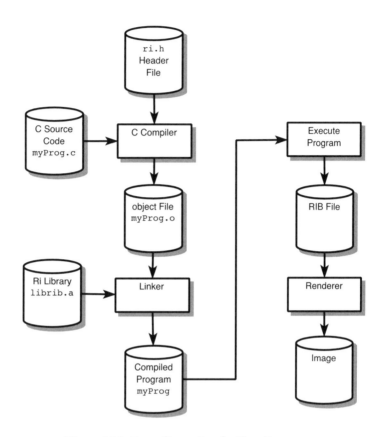

Figure 16.1 Compiling a RenderMan C program.

Of course it is also perfectly practical to generate RIBs by simply printing out the relevant commands. Though this may appear a little simpler at first, using the official functions provides an additional level of error checking, and flexibility.

A first C program

A RenderMan client program must call the function RiBegin() before any other RenderMan function in order to initialize the renderer, and it must end by calling RiEnd(). Between these function calls you can execute rendering commands by calling functions whose names are the same as those found in RIBs with the prefix Ri (Rendering Interface) attached. For example a sphere is created by the function RiSphere(). A C program that will generate our first RIB file (Listing 6.1) is shown in Listing 16.1.

Listing 16.1 A simple C program.

```
/* min.c - a minimal C program to use RenderMan */

#include <ri.h>

int main(int argc, char *argv[])
{
RiBegin(RI_NULL);
    RiDisplay ("min.tiff","file","rgb",RI_NULL);
    RiProjection ("perspective",RI_NULL);
    RiWorldBegin();
        RiTranslate(0,0,2);
        RiSphere(1,-1,1,360,RI_NULL);
    RiWorldEnd();
RiEnd();
return 0;
}
```

As there is a direct correspondence between RIB commands and C functions, all of the previous techniques described in RIB form can be applied in C. The C API is more flexible, however, as we can use C code to generate RIBs that are far more complex than you could ever hope to produce by hand. For example, to generate a RIB similar to Listing 15.4, which we used to explore depth of field, you would use a for loop as in Listing 16.2. To extend the line of spheres indefinitely is trivial in the C code, but incredibly tedious using RIB.

Listing 16.2 Using a for loop.

```
/* loop.c - Create a line of Spheres */

#include <ri.h>

int main(int argc, char *argv[])
{
```

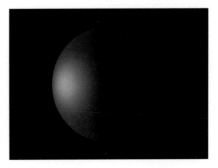

Figure 11.1 Pointlight.

Figure 11.3 Distantlight.

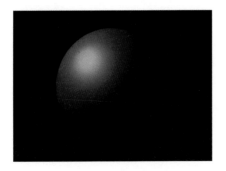

Figure 11.4 Spotlight.

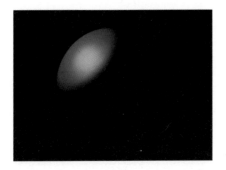

Figure 11.6 Softening the edge of a spot.

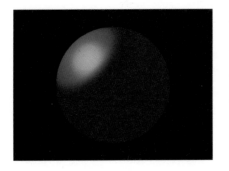

Figure 11.8 Ambient and spotlight.

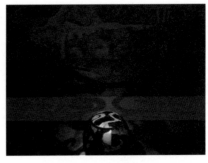

A textured scene.

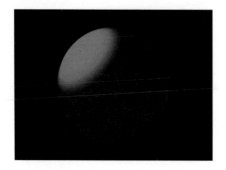

Figure 12.2 The "matte" shader.

Figure 12.3 The "metal" shader.

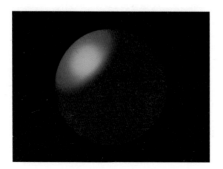

Figure 12.4 The "plastic" shader.

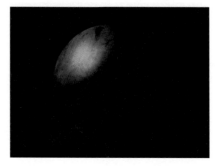

Figure 12.6 The "paintedplastic" shader

The HSV colour space.

Blending two colours.

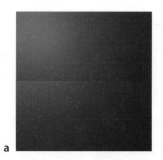

Creating bands.

A soft edge.

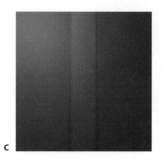

A vertical line.

Layering two effects.

A disk.

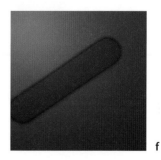

Arbitrary lines.

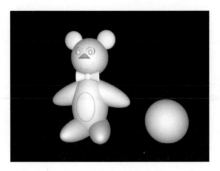

Figure 8.7 John the Bear.

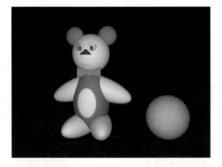

Figure 9.5 John the Bear in colour.

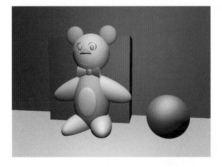

Figure 13.9 John the Bear with flat
surfaces and shading added.

Images derived from the RIB file 'bear.rib' (courtesy of Frederic Cervini).

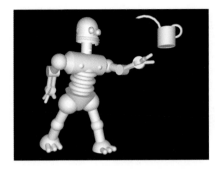

Figure 8.6 *A robot created using only simple surfaces.*

Figure 12.7 *The robot scene with lighting and shading.*

The finished scene.

Images derived from the RIB file 'robot.rib' (courtesy of Faan van Tonder).

Figure 24.9 *A reflective surface.*

Figure 26.9 *Using turbulence with a spline.*

Figure 28.2 *An anisotropic surface.*

Figure 28.3 *Reorienting the satin shader.*

Jelly Bean Town, rendered with Air (image courtesy of AMI AG (Asset Media International AG)).

Nutcrackers, rendered with Air (image courtesy of Haggi Flöser).

Using depth of field (images courtesy of Kevan Shorey).

*Joe's Playtime, rendered with PRMan
(image courtesy of Kevan Shorey).*

*Emily and the snail, rendered with PRMan
(image courtesy of Kevan Shorey).*

Hut on the rocks, rendered with PRMan. Image fom Harry Potter and the Philosopher's Stone. © 2001 Warner Bros. All rights reserved. Visual effects by the Moving Picture Company (MPC).

*South African wines, rendered with RenderDrive. © Theseus Projects.
(Courtesy of Advanced Rendering Technology.)*

*Aircraft interior, rendered with RenderDrive. © Bombadier Aerospace
Inc. (Courtesy of Advanced Rendering Technology.)*

Jaguar X400, rendered with RenderDrive. © Burrows, Essex.
(Courtesy of Jaguar Cars and Advanced Rendering Technology.)

V6 engine, rendered with RenderDrive. © Burrows, Essex.
(Courtesy of Jaguar Cars and Advanced Rendering Technology.)

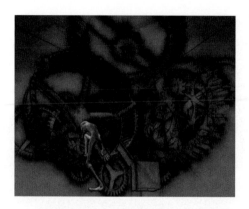

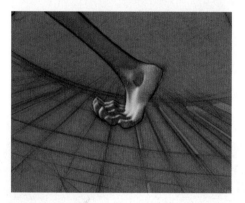

Images from "a flat pack project". Reproduced with permission.

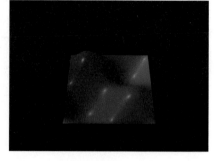

Figure 17.3 *Changing the colour of points.*

Figure 17.4 *Blending colours on other surfaces.*

Dust transport, rendered with PRMan.

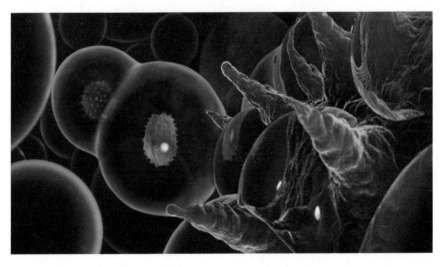

Water drops, rendered with PRMan.

Images from BBC series 'Weather'.
Visual effects by the Moving Picture Company (MPC).

Flowers, rendered with Air (image courtesy of Haggi Flöser).

```
int i;
RiBegin(RI_NULL);
    RiDisplay ("loop.tiff", "file", "rgb",RI_NULL);
    RiProjection ("perspective",RI_NULL);
    RiDepthOfField(2.8,0.100,2);
    RiTranslate(0,0,1);
    RiWorldBegin();
        RiTranslate(0.3,0,0);
        for(i=0;i<12;i++)
            {
            RiSphere(0.25,-0.25,0.25,360,RI_NULL);
            RiTranslate(-0.2,0,0.5);
            }
    RiWorldEnd();
RiEnd();
return 0;
}
```

Parameter lists

The C language has a far more complex syntax than the RIB file format which is simply a list of explicit commands. Because of the increased flexibility, the C API can't always guess what we're trying to do in the same way as the renderer can, and hence it occasionally needs extra hints.

In particular, parameter lists such as the points of a polygon or parameters of a shader are somewhat tricky to handle. As in RIB files, a C parameter list consists of tokens (parameter names) and values (arrays of data). In C, however, values are always passed to the renderer through pointers, which can produce somewhat convoluted code. Typically an array is created which contains the values, and then the array is passed to the Ri function.

The C language also needs some method of knowing how many different parameters are in each list, and this is done by terminating each list with the predefined token RI_NULL. Great care must be taken to include this, as failure to do so will produce unexpected results. Many commands that we have already used do support parameter lists even though we may have safely ignored them when using the RIB API, and hence RI_NULL appears frequently in the code. Listing 16.3 demonstrates a simple parameter list which we've used to create a linear patch similar to that in Listing 13.4.

Listing 16.3 Passing a parameter list.

```
/* param.c - create a linear patch to demonstrate
            parameter lists */

#include <ri.h>

int main(int argc, char *argv[])
{
RtPoint square[4]={{0,0,0},{1,0,0},{0,1,0},{1,1,0}};
RtColor red={1,0,0};
float fov=30;

RiBegin(RI_NULL);
    RiDisplay ("param.tiff", "file", "rgb",RI_NULL);
    RiProjection ("perspective",
                  "fov",&fov,
                  RI_NULL);
    RiTranslate(-0.5,-0.5,3);
    RiWorldBegin();
        RiColor(red);
        RiPatch("bilinear",
                "P",square,
                RI_NULL);
    RiWorldEnd();
RiEnd();
return 0;
}
```

Listing 16.3 also uses a parameter to specify the field of view. You should note that even though "fov" only takes a single float value it is still passed via a pointer. Colours are passed using the type RtColor, which is, again, actually an array.

Declaring parameter types

In the case of the patch used in Listing 16.3, it is relatively clear that the array "P" must contain four elements, each being a point. In many cases, however, there may be no way of interpreting a parameter without additional information. For example, a shader which takes a parameter "x", might define "x" as either a colour or a float, or even an array of floats. The only way to determine this would be by reference to the shader itself.

While most renderers are capable of extracting this information, you usually need to provide the C API with a hint to tell it how to handle each value passed into it. The function RiDeclare can be used to specify the type of a variable before it is passed through the C API. This is demonstrated in Listing 16.4 where the surface shader "myConstantSurface", requires a parameter "customColor" of type "uniform color". You can usually find the correct type of variable by reference to documentation or shader source.

Listing 16.4 Declaring a parameter type.

```
/*declare.c - declare the type of a parameter
            to a custom shader */

#include <ri.h>

int main(int argc, char *argv[])
{
RtPoint square[4]={{0,0,0},{1,0,0},{0,1,0},{1,1,0}};
RtColor red={1,0,0};
float fov=30;

RiBegin(RI_NULL);
    RiDisplay ("declare.tiff", "file", "rgb",RI_NULL);
    RiProjection ("perspective",
                "fov",&fov,
                RI_NULL);
    RiTranslate(-0.5,-0.5,3);
    RiWorldBegin();
        RiDeclare("customColor", "uniform color");
        RiSurface("myConstantSurface",
                "customColor",red,
                RI_NULL);
        RiPatch("bilinear",
                "P",square,
```

```
                RI_NULL);
    RiWorldEnd();
RiEnd();
return 0;
}
```

Declare is also available in the RIB API, though depending on your renderer you may not be required to use it.

Certain other functions explicitly require similar hints as additional parameters. For example, the Polygon RIB command can work out for itself the number of points in the polygon, but the C equivalent RiPolygon function requires the number of vertices as its first parameter.

Light sources

When you declare light sources in a RIB file you must specify a handle, so that you can refer to the same light later in the file. The C API uses the same concept but rather than the user providing their own handle, the handle is calculated by the RiLightSource() function and passed back to the user as a variable of type RtLightHandle. To create a light you therefore need to use code like that in Listing 16.5.

Listing 16.5 Declaring a light.

```
/* light.c - create a light source */

#include <ri.h>

int main(int argc, char *argv[])
{
RtPoint square[4]={{0,0,0},{1,0,0},{0,1,0},{1,1,0}};
RtPoint lightPos[1]={{0,0,-0.2}};
RtLightHandle theLight;
RtColor red={1,0,0};
float fov=30;

RiBegin(RI_NULL);
    RiDisplay ("light.tiff", "file", "rgb",RI_NULL);
```

```
    RiProjection ("perspective",
                  "fov",&fov,
                  RI_NULL);
  RiTranslate(-0.5,-0.5,3);
  RiWorldBegin();
      theLight=RiLightSource("pointlight",
                             "from",lightPos,
                             RI_NULL);

      RiColor(red);
      RiPatch("bilinear",
              "P",square,
              RI_NULL);
  RiWorldEnd();
RiEnd();
return 0;
}
```

Suggested activities

Investigate whether your renderer provides a C API library and suitable header files. Does this generate RIB or render directly (either, both or neither may be available)? Compile the examples, and examine the RIB files generated.

Consider which aspects of your scene could have been generated more easily using the C API.

Summary

```
RiBegin(RI_NULL);
RiEnd();
RiSphere(rad,zmin,zmax,theta,...,RI_NULL);
RiPatch("type",...,RI_NULL);
RiPolygon(nverts,...,RI_NULL);
RiColor(color);
RiDeclare("varName","varType");
RtLightHandle l=RiLightSource("type",...,RI_NULL);
```

Chapter 17

Particles and Hair

Introduction

When modelling dust, explosions, fur, hair and other similar phenomena we often require not hundreds of surfaces but perhaps tens or hundreds of thousands. In order to deal with these demands Points and Curves primitives were added to the RenderMan standard. In this chapter we'll look at how you can use these to describe objects, which are too fine to require a full 3D model, in a highly efficient manner.

Particles

Particles are one of the most commonly used tools in the special effects industry, creating smoke, fire, dust, rain and countless other phenomena. These illusions rely not on the appearance of the individual particles but rather the combined image of thousands of particles or more. While it is possible to render each of these particles as a simple object such as a sphere, the Points command is designed to render a complete particle system as a single piece of geometry, and in doing so greatly improves efficiency.

Because particles are designed to be used in huge numbers it makes little sense to create them by hand in a RIB file. Using the C API, however, it is trivial to create any number of points. In Listing 17.1 we fill the array "position" with 1000 coordinates generated by sine and cosine waves of different frequencies. In the second half of the code we simply pass this to the Points command using the "P" parameter. As we're using the C API we also need to specify how many points there are, but from a RIB file this is not necessary. We've added a point light and a metal shading model to produce Figure 17.1.

Listing 17.1 The Points command.

```
/* point.c - create a simple Particle System */

#include <ri.h>
#include <math.h>

#define COUNT 1000

float jitter(float scale)
{
    float val=random()%1000;
    return (val/500-1)*scale;
}

int main(int argc, char *argv[])
{
RtPoint position[COUNT];
RtColor red={1,0,0};
float fov=30;
int i;

/*Generate Particle Postions*/
for(i=0;i<COUNT;i++)
    {
    position[i][0]=sin(i*0.5)*50+jitter(2);
    position[i][1]=cos(i*0.1)*50+jitter(2);
    position[i][2]=cos(i*0.5)*100+jitter(2);
    }

RiBegin(RI_NULL);
    RiDisplay ("point.tiff", "file", "rgb",RI_NULL);
    RiProjection ("perspective",
                "fov",&fov,
                RI_NULL);
    RiWorldBegin();
        RiTranslate(0,0,300);
        RiColor(red);
        RiPoints(COUNT,
                "P",position,
                RI_NULL);
    RiWorldEnd();
RiEnd();
return 0;
}
```

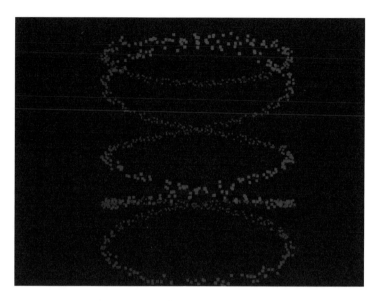

Figure 17.1 The Points *command.*

Particle size

By default, particles have a width of 1, and hence in Listing 17.1 we had to translate the particles system back from the camera by 300 units to ensure that the particles were sufficiently small. In Listing 17.2, however, we've taken control over the size of the particles. We've created two sets of points here, and in the first – which is coloured red – we've set the size of particles using the parameter "constant width". This sets a uniform size for every point in the group, however, and you may need to set the size of each point individually. We've done this in the case of the second (green) set of points using the parameter "width", which requires a size for each particle. The resulting image is shown in Figure 17.2, again with appropriate lighting.

Listing 17.2 Controlling the size of points.

```c
/* width.c - Create Particles of different sizes*/

#define COUNT 2000

int main(int argc, char *argv[])
{
RtPoint position[COUNT];
RtColor red={1,0,0};
RtColor green={0,1,0};
float width[COUNT];
float constantwidth=0.5;
float fov=30;
int i;

/*Generate Particle Postions*/
for(i=0;i<COUNT;i++)
    {
    position[i][0]=sin(i*0.5)*50+jitter(2);
    position[i][1]=cos(i*0.1)*50+jitter(2);
    position[i][2]=cos(i*0.5)*100+jitter(2);
    width[i]=jitter(0.5)+0.5;
    }

RiBegin(RI_NULL);
    RiDisplay ("width.tiff", "file", "rgb",RI_NULL);
    RiProjection ("perspective",
                    "fov",&fov,
                    RI_NULL);
    RiWorldBegin();
        RiTranslate(0,0,300);
        RiColor(red);
        RiPoints(COUNT/2,
                    "P",position,
                    "constantwidth", &constantwidth,
                    RI_NULL);
        RiColor(green);
        RiPoints(COUNT/2,
                    "P",position+COUNT/2,
                    "width",width+COUNT/2,
                    RI_NULL);
    RiWorldEnd();
RiEnd();
return 0;
}
```

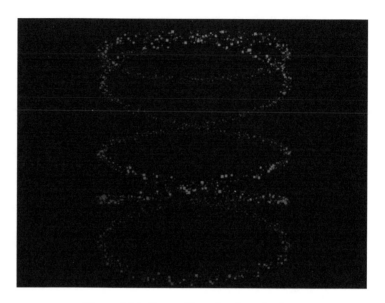

Figure 17.2 Controlling the size of points.

"Width" is just one example of a varying parameter. This allows us to specify a width for each point in the particle system. You can use the same approach to give each point a unique colour, by supplying a varying value of Cs (the shading language name for the surface colour). This replaces the uniform colour specified by the Color command with a colour for each point. We've done this in Listing 17.3 to produce the image in Figure 17.3. In fact you can do this for any kind of object, allowing you to have a colour which changes gradually over the surface (Listing 17.4 and Figure 17.4).

Listing 17.3 Changing the colour of points.

```c
/* color.c - Create Particles of different colors*/

#include <ri.h>
#include <math.h>

#define COUNT 2000

int main(int argc, char *argv[])
{
RtPoint position[COUNT];
RtColor color[COUNT];
float constantwidth=0.5;
float fov=30;
int i;

/*Generate Particle Postions*/
for(i=0;i<COUNT;i++)
    {
    position[i][0]=sin(i*0.5)*50+jitter(2);
    position[i][1]=cos(i*0.1)*50+jitter(2);
    position[i][2]=cos(i*0.5)*100+jitter(2);
    color[i][0]=jitter(0.5)+0.5;
    color[i][1]=jitter(0.5)+0.5;
    color[i][2]=jitter(0.5)+0.5;
    }

RiBegin(RI_NULL);
    RiDisplay ("color.tiff", "file", "rgb",RI_NULL);
    RiProjection ("perspective",
                  "fov",&fov,
                  RI_NULL);
    RiWorldBegin();
        RiTranslate(0,0,300);
        RiPoints(COUNT,
                 "P",position,
                 "constantwidth", &constantwidth,
                 "Cs",color,
                 RI_NULL);
    RiWorldEnd();
RiEnd();
return 0;
}
```

Figure 17.3 *Changing the colour of points (also Plate XIV).*

Listing 17.4 Blending colours on other surfaces.

```
#cubic.rib
Display "cubic.tiff" "file" "rgb"
Projection "perspective" "fov" [ 30 ]

Translate -0.5 -0.5 3

WorldBegin
        LightSource "ambientlight" 1 "intensity" [ 0.1]
        LightSource "pointlight" 2
                "from" [-2 2 -2]
                "intensity" [ 10 ]

        Surface "plastic"
        Rotate 40 1 0 0

  Patch "bicubic" "P" [ 0 0   0 0.4 0    0 0.6 0    0 1 0   0
                        0 0.4 0 0.4 0.4  3 0.6 0.4 -3 1 0.4 0
                        0 0.6 0 0.4 0.6 -3 0.6 0.6  3 1 0.6 0
                        0 1   0 0.4 1    0 0.6 1    0 1 1   0]
                "Cs" [ 1 0   0 0   1    0 0   0    1 1 1   1]
WorldEnd
```

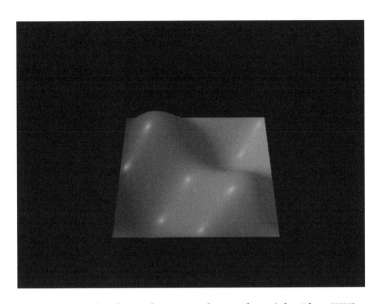

Figure 17.4 *Blending colours on other surfaces (also Plate XIV).*

If you look closely you might notice that points are not rendered as true 3D objects but as small, flat flakes, which are oriented towards the camera. This is one of the optimizations which allows thousands of particles to be rendered in only a few seconds. Although the individual points are rather limited in their appearance, the intention is that points should be visible only as a cloud, not as individuals. Even though points are actually flat you can still scale, rotate and translate them as if they were real 3D objects – their flatness is an optimization which should go unnoticed. However, you must avoid making them too large on screen or else this subterfuge will be uncovered.

Hair

Rendering hair or fur has much in common with particle techniques. Once again the visual interest comes not from the complexity of the individual objects but from the large number of objects that compose an image. The Curves command takes the idea of a flat object oriented to the camera, as used for particles and extends it to render a set of curves. A curve has a length, but it has no depth, and minimal width.

We've created a set of curves in Listing 17.5. As was the case for points, we first calculate the positions of the point on each curve and store them into an array. If you wanted to create a realistic hair simulation (see back cover image), then the complexity would lie here, in calculating the movement of the hairs, rather than in the rendering itself. The curves we have created are quite simple, and each contain four points. However, as it is possible to specify different numbers of points for each curve in a set, we also create an array nverts that we will use to tell the renderer how many points belong to this particular curve.

Listing 17.5 The Curves command.

```
/* curves.c - create a set of curves */

#include <ri.h>
#include <math.h>

#define COUNT 1000

float jitter(float scale)
{
    float val=random()%1000;
    return (val/500-1)*scale;
}

int main(int argc, char *argv[])
{
RtPoint position[COUNT*4];
RtInt nverts[COUNT];
RtColor red={1,0,0};
float curveWidth=0.3;
float fov=30;
int i;

/*Generate Curve Postions*/
for(i=0;i<COUNT;i++)
    {
```

```
        float tx=(sin(i*0.3)*i*50)/COUNT+jitter(5);
        float ty=(cos(i*0.3)*i*50)/COUNT+jitter(5);

        position[i*4+0][0]=0;
        position[i*4+0][1]=0;
        position[i*4+0][2]=50;

        position[i*4+1][0]=0.1*tx;
        position[i*4+1][1]=0.1*ty;
        position[i*4+1][2]=25;

        position[i*4+2][0]=0.4*tx;
        position[i*4+2][1]=0.4*ty;
        position[i*4+2][2]=0;

        position[i*4+3][0]=tx;
        position[i*4+3][1]=ty;
        position[i*4+3][2]=-25;

        nverts[i]=4;
        }
RiBegin(RI_NULL);
    RiDisplay ("curves.tiff", "file", "rgb",RI_NULL);
    RiProjection ("perspective",
                    "fov",&fov,
                    RI_NULL);
    RiWorldBegin();
        RiTranslate(0,0,200);
        RiColor(red);
        RiRotate(45,1,0,0);
        RiCurves("linear",COUNT, nverts, "nonperiodic",
                "P",position,
                "constantwidth",&curveWidth,
                RI_NULL);
    RiWorldEnd();
RiEnd();
return 0;
}
```

Like patches, we can choose to either connect these points with straight lines or fit a curve through them. The first parameter to the Curves command is therefore either "linear" or "cubic". We then tell the renderer the number of curves, and number of points in each curve, as we've previously calculated. It is possible to connect the end of a curve back to its start making a small loop, but here we have specified that the curves should be non-periodic. Finally we pass in the array of points previously calculated. Like points, we can specify the width of the curve using the parameters "constantwidth" or "width". The resulting image is shown in Figure 17.5.

Figure 17.5 *The* Curves *command.*

Suggested activities

Check your renderer's support for Points and Curves.

Write a simple C program to create particle systems to simulate dust or smoke. Add the generated RIB commands into a scene that you have created.

Create a set of curves, and render them out over several frames. Displace the curves slightly at each time step to simulate the effect of wind.

Summary

RIB API

```
Points ...
Curves "linear" [nvertices] "non-periodic" ...
```

C API

```
RiPoints(nPoints, ..., RI_NULL);
RiCurves("linear", ncurves,
    nvertices[], "nonperiodic", ...,RI_NULL),
```

Part

3

Shading

Though RenderMan supports a wide range of modelling primitives, it would be impossible to use geometry to create the level of detail required by even the simplest of scenes. Instead, fine surface detail is added to coarser base surfaces through the use of shaders. You can use RenderMan shaders to influence many stages of the rendering process, but the most common form is the surface shader. The job of the surface shader is to decide the colour of each point on a surface, based upon its position, orientation, lighting and the observer. The renderer provides the shader with the necessary information to make this decision, and then integrates the result into the final image.

In order to maximize flexibility, shaders take the form of short fragments of computer code. While obviously being able to program helps here, a small amount of knowledge goes a long way, as most of the hard work is already being done by the renderer. Shaders tend to be very short, and algorithmically simple. Even simple shaders can produce visually interesting surfaces.

Chapter 18

My First Shader

Introduction

In this section we will compile and view a simple shader. In doing so you will become familiar with the shader writing tools and processes, which we will apply to more complex examples in later chapters.

The development process

Shaders are written using a special programming language know as SL (Shading Language). A shader called `myShader` will typically be found in the file "`myShader.sl`". While this isn't strictly necessary, it is a very sensible convention to adopt, and we'll assume it here.

In order to use the shader with a particular renderer it first needs to be compiled, and this is done using a program supplied with the renderer. We'll use the command "`shader`" here, but that command should be substituted for whatever is required by your renderer. You would therefore compile your new surface "`myShader`" using the command "`shader myShader.sl`"

This will either produce a list of errors indicating there's a problem with the code contained in the file `myShader.sl`, or it will produce a shader object file. This will generally be called `myShader` with an extension that varies depending on which compiler you've used. In the case of PRMan the file would be "`myShader.slo`".

At this stage it would be possible to go into the modelling package of your choice, and use the shader. During the process of writing a shader, however, you'll probably need to do this hundreds of times. It therefore makes sense to streamline the process as much as possible (and also avoid tying up a potentially valuable modelling licence). A good method of doing this is to either manually or using your modeller create a RIB file which has the new shader attached to a simple object (a sphere or a plane). This can be rendered quickly and easily from the command line, and simple geometry allows you to understand the behaviour of your shader better than a complex model would.

The development process therefore becomes:

- **edit** myShader.sl
- shader myShader.sl
- render testMyShader.rib
- viewer testMyShader.tiff
- rinse and repeat...

The process can further be optimized on UNIX platforms by using a Makefile. The make program is also available for non-UNIX platforms but is not a standard feature. Obtaining it is highly recommended. Having edited the shader, simply typing "make" will compile the shader, render the test image, and view the results. Such a Makefile is shown in Listing 18.1.

Listing 18.1 Shader Makefile.

```
RENDER=angel
SLCOMPILER=giles
VIEWER=viewer
SLEXT=slc

SHADERNAME=first

all : ${SHADERNAME}.tiff
      ${VIEWER} ${SHADERNAME}.tiff

${SHADERNAME}.tiff : ${SHADERNAME}.${SLEXT} test.rib
      cat test.rib | sed s/XXXX/${SHADERNAME}/g | ${RENDER}

${SHADERNAME}.${SLEXT} : ${SHADERNAME}.sl
      ${SLCOMPILER} ${SHADERNAME}.sl

clean :
      rm -f *.tiff *.slc
```

The first few lines of the Makefile define the tools to be used to compile and render the image. To test a different shader you should change the line SHADERNAME=myShader to something more appropriate. The Makefile renders the RIB file test.rib, which should contain code similar to that in Listing 18.2, modifying it dynamically to attach the shader under test to the object.

Listing 18.2 Shader test RIB.

```
Display "XXXX.tiff" "file" "rgb"
Format 320 240 1
Projection "perspective" "fov" [45]
LightSource "ambientlight" 1
                            "intensity" [0.2]
LightSource "spotlight" 2
                            "from" [-1 1 0 ]
                            "to" [0 0 3]
                            "intensity" [3]
Translate 0 0 3
WorldBegin
            Color [1 0 0]
            Surface "XXXX"
            Sphere 1 -1 1 360
WorldEnd
```

A typical shader development process might use a simple RIB file for 50 per cent of development, a more complex RIB, perhaps containing the target surface so it can be seen in situ for the next 40 per cent of the time, and full renders for the final 10 per cent when the shader is being fine tuned.

Writing the code

The code for our first shader is in Listing 18.3. The first line indicates that this is a shader of type "surface" and has the name "first". This is the name that it will be referred to by in a RIB file or animation package. The rest of the file will be considered in greater detail in the following chapter.

Listing 18.3 A first shader.

```
surface first()
    {
    Oi=Os;
    Ci=Cs*Oi;
    }
```

The shader source code is simply text, and can be entered using any text editor. It should be saved in a text file with the name "first.sl", then compiled using the command "shader first.sl" to create a file "first.slo". Generate a RIB file called first.rib, which has the shader "first" attached to an object, and then "render   first.rib". Alternatively, using the above Makefile and RIB, change SHADERNAME to "first", and type make. In either case you should be rewarded by an image showing an object with a constant colour, similar to Figure 19.1.

Figure 18.1 A first shader.

Suggested activities

Check your renderer's documentation to establish the command required to compile a shader, and work out what the file name of the compiled shader will be.

Compile and view the simple shader in whatever rendering systems are available to you.

Summary

The shader development process is summarized in Figure 18.2.

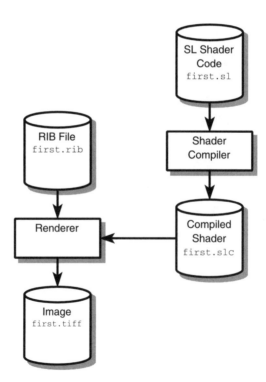

Figure 18.2 Compiling shaders.

Chapter 19

Lighting Models

Introduction

Having successfully written and rendered a simple shader, we're now ready to start expanding the body of the code, to produce more interesting results. In this chapter we'll investigate the way that the surface interacts with the lights in the scene. You'll see that some simple approximations will allow us to produce a wide range of effects that you can use as a starting point for your own shaders.

Constant

The shader "first", from the previous chapter, is in fact identical to one of the standard RenderMan shaders, known as "constant". This ignores any lights in the scene, and simply applies a flat colour to the object, the colour used being that specified in the RIB file. The opacity of the object is also considered.

If we examine the code for "constant" more closely (Listing 20.1), it uses four variables Oi, Os, Cs and Ci. O is for opacity and C is for colour. Os and Cs are the values assigned by the Color and Opacity commands in the RIB file. These are passed to the shader by the renderer. It is the surfaces shader's job to take these values and calculate the colour and opacity of the object when it is observed from a particular position. The values calculated are assigned to the variables Oi and Ci, which are then used by the renderer in the rest of its processing. These standard variables are known as "globals", and are the standard mechanism by which data flows into and out of the shader (a summary of these is provided on the inside back cover).

Listing 19.1 The constant shader.

```
surface constant ()
{
    Oi = Os;
    Ci = Oi * Cs;
}
```

The `Constant` shader simply takes the provided opacity (`Os`) and assigns it to the output opacity (`Oi`). The second line where the output colour (`Ci`) is calculated is slightly more complex, as the output colour is the input colour multiplied by the opacity. This is known as "pre-multiplied" or "associated" opacity. Normally, colour values range between 0 and 1, so `1,0,0` would be bright red. However, if this colour was applied to a surface that was totally transparent, then the surface couldn't carry any colour at all (`0,0,0`). If the surface was 50 per cent transparent, then half the output colour would come from the surface (`0.5,0,0`) and half would be from whatever was behind the surface. Multiplying the surface colour by the opacity takes this into account. It also makes some of the renderer's calculations simpler to handle colours in this format, but the simple rule is that you should always multiply the output colour by the opacity.

Matte

In order to make a surface appear three dimensional we need a surface shader that will take into account the position of lights and the orientation of the surface to these lights.

Surface orientation

The orientation of a surface at a point is defined by the surface normal, which is stored in the global variable `N`. This variable has a different value at every point on the surface, and contains a vector which points away from the surface. We're also going to need to consider the orientation from which the surface is being viewed, and this is in the variable `I`. Both `N` and `I` are illustrated in Figure 19.1.

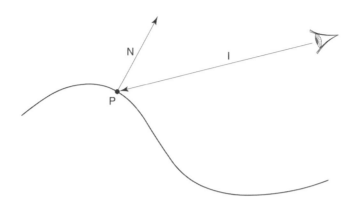

Figure 19.1 N *and* I.

The variable N also tells us which side of the surface is the front and which is the back, but we probably don't care – we want to shade the back just the same as the front. We therefore need to calculate the "face forward surface normal" – we simply reverse the direction of N if it is pointing away from us (in the same direction as I), and store it in a new variable "Nf" which we know is pointing towards us. We do this using the function faceforwards():

```
normal Nf=faceforwards(N,I);
```

Nf is declared as a variable of type "normal", since although it is a vector we are going to store a surface normal in it. Normals behave slightly differently to ordinary vectors when certain operations are performed on them, and the compiler may also use this information to detect potential errors in your code. Old implementations of RenderMan simply used the type "point" for all vectors, and this is still reflected in some documentation but in modern code "point" should only be used to represent a position in space.

Depending on your implementation, you may have to declare all variables at the beginning of your code (as in C) or you may be able to declare variables immediately before you need them (as in C++). While the former style is more portable, inline declarations can make short examples more readable. Should your compiler have problems, simply separate the declaration and move it to the top of the shader code:

```
normal Nf;
...
Nf=faceforwards(N,I);
```

The variable Nf is given the value of N, flipped (if necessary) so that it is facing towards the observer. When we use this line in a shader (Listing 19.2) we also need to normalize the vector N. The length of the vector N has no meaning, and hence by convention it should be set to be of unit length. Using normals of non-unit length can generate unpredictable results when they are passed to built-in functions. Note that normalize and normal are completely unrelated concepts which unfortunately happen to share similar names.

Listing 19.2 A diffuse shader.

```
surface second ()
{
    normal Nf = faceforward (normalize(N),I);
    Oi = Os;
    Ci = Cs * diffuse(Nf) * Oi;
}
```

Collecting light

In our second shader the variable Nf is passed to the predefined function diffuse(). This does all the work of collecting light from sources in the scene and calculating the illumination of the surface. As it takes a surface normal but not the observer's position (I) the colour returned models a rough surface which scatters light in all directions equally (Figure 19.2).

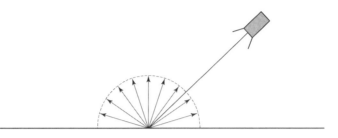

Figure 19.2 Diffuse scattering.

The value returned by diffuse is not simply the amplitude of the lights but also the colour. However, one of the benefits of SL over C is that it knows about colours and other variable types. It is therefore perfectly reasonable to add together or multiply colours, and the results will be correct.

The "second" shader corresponds to the standard shader "matte" which is defined in Listing 19.3. In addition to diffuse lighting, the contribution from any ambient light is included by the call to ambient() to ensure that the dark sides of objects aren't completely black. The collected light is multiplied by the surface colour and by Oi then assigned to the output Ci to produce a surface which looks like Figure 19.3.

Listing 19.3 The matte shader.

```
surface matte (
            float Ka = 1;
            float Kd = 1;
            )
{
    normal Nf = faceforward (normalize(N),I);

    Oi = Os;
    Ci = Oi * Cs * (Ka * ambient() + Kd * diffuse(Nf));
}
```

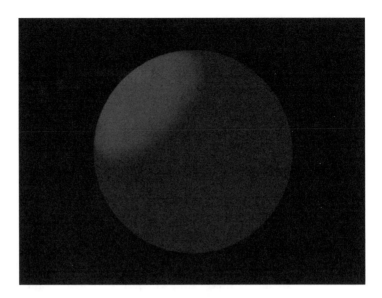

Figure 19.3 *The matte shader.*

Matte also has two parameters "Ka" and "Kd", which control the contributions from diffuse and ambient lighting. These can be assigned by parameter list in the RIB file (and typically in the modeller), allowing the shader's appearance to be modified by an animator without having to modify the code. To create such a parameter you must not only declare the parameters but provide default value. If no value is provided by the user then these values will be used.

Metal

Matte models a rough surface which scatters light, but real surfaces often reflect light in a more coherent fashion. When you view a metallic surface from the correct angle light will be reflected directly towards you creating a bright "specular" highlight. Depending on the texture of the surface this highlight may be bright and sharply defined, or more evenly spread over a large area. Such reflections are illustrated in Figure 19.4.

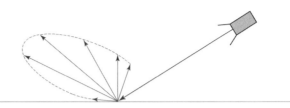

Figure 19.4 Specular reflection.

This form of reflection is modelled by the function specular(). In order to calculate the amount of light being reflected in a particular direction we will need to tell it the surface normal, the roughness of the surface, and the direction for which it is required to calculate a reflection.

The direction of the required refection is typically stored in a variable called V and while unlike Ci, Cs, N and other globals, the use of the name V is purely a convention. The adoption of standard names for commonly used information makes shaders easier to read. Nf is also a commonly adopted name to mean the face forwards surface normal. V is the direction back towards the observer, so we simply add the line:

```
vector V=normalize(-I);
```

as I is the vector from the observer to the point on the surface. V is of type vector as it is a free vector with no special properties other than indicating a direction.

In Listing 19.4, in place of diffuse(), the function specular has been called, resulting in a highlight which is dependent on the observer's position as well as the position of the light.

Listing 19.4 A specular shader.

```
surface third ()
{
    normal Nf = faceforward (normalize(N),I);
    vector V = -normalize(I);

    Oi = Os;
    Ci = Oi * Cs * specular(Nf,V,0.1);
}
```

This shader models the appearance of a rough metal surface, and is closely related to the standard RenderMan shader "metal" which is listed in Listing 19.5. Once again the standard version adds an ambient contribution, along with controls to let an end user modify the surface. The resulting image is shown in Figure 19.5.

Listing 19.5 The metal shader.

```
surface metal (
        float Ka = 1;
        float Ks = 1;
        float roughness = .1;)
{
    normal Nf = faceforward (normalize(N),I);
    vector V = -normalize(I);

    Oi = Os;
    Ci = Oi * Cs * (Ka*ambient() + Ks*specular(Nf,V,
roughness));
}
```

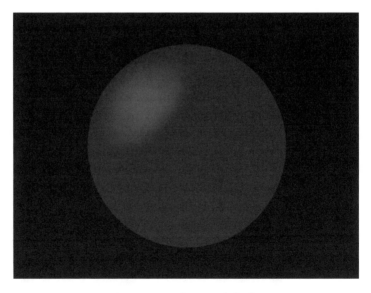

Figure 19.5 The metal shader.

Plastic

In practice, most surfaces combine some degree of both a diffuse and a specular highlight as in Figure 19.6. This was produced using the standard shader "plastic" in Listing 19.6, which combines the functionality of both matte and metal.

Listing 19.6 The plastic shader.

```
surface plastic (
        float Ka = 1;
        float Kd = .5;
        float Ks = .5;
        float roughness = .1;
        color specularcolor = 1;)
{
    normal Nf = faceforward (normalize(N),I);
    vector V = -normalize(I);

    Oi = Os;
    Ci = Oi * ( Cs * (Ka*ambient() + Kd*diffuse(Nf)) +
        specularcolor * Ks*specular(Nf,V,roughness));
}
```

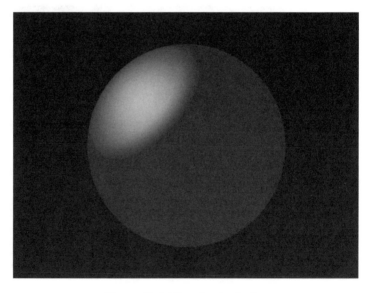

Figure 19.6 The plastic shader.

In the plastic shader the RIB colour `Cs` is used to control the colour of the diffuse lighting, while the colour of the specular highlight is controlled by the parameter `specularcolor`. This models plastic relatively well for reasons discussed in Chapter 12. By adjusting the weighting parameters (`Ka`, `Kd` and `Ks`) and changing `specularcolor`, however, it is possible to reproduce any of the effects of matte or metal. For this reason plastic forms the starting point from which most shaders are developed.

Suggested activities

Examine objects around you to establish their reflective properties. Look for specular highlights and consider if that is related to the base colour or separately defined.

Compile and view each of the shaders, noting the differences between them. Try adjusting the parameters of the plastic model to more closely match surfaces you see around you.

Summary

`Cs, Os` – input colour and opacity
`Ci, Oi` – output colour and opacity
`diffuse(N)`
`specular(N,V,roughness)`

Related functions

phong(N,V,size)

Though it is little used, SL also supports the `Phong` shading model, which behaves much like `specular`. The choice is an aesthetic one, but `specular()` is usually preferred.

Chapter

20

Colour Ramps

Introduction

Having established a basic technique for lighting our object we can now move on to the task of creating variations across the surface. In this section we introduce the most basic of such variations – a ramp of colour changing smoothly from one side of the object to the other.

A standard shader

Though the whole process of calculating the colour of a surface point is referred to as shading, and in RenderMan any custom code written in SL is known as a shader, the term shading more strictly refers to the calculation of the interaction of light with the surface. Though a little cliched the standard plastic model provides reasonable flexibility when used intelligently and hence we may consider the actual shading part of our shader as done. In fact what most shaders are concerned with is the variation of properties such as colour and roughness, across the surface (which we will refer to as texturing). It is these variations which we will use to create visual interest, and make rendered images spring to life rather than appearing dull and artificial.

If you consider the plastic model as a black box, then each of the variables it uses (`Ka`, `Kd`, `Ks`, `Cs`, `Os`, `specularcolor`, `Nf`, `V` and `roughness`) is an input and the variables `Ci`, and `Oi` are its outputs. In the standard shaders most of the input variables are constant across the whole surface but you can manipulate any of them to create a more realistic image. At the very least you would expect a surface to have some variation in colour. Based on this premise, we can create a standard shader that we can use as a template for further shader development. Such a starting point is shown in Listing 20.1.

Listing 20.1 A standard shader template.

```
surface standard (
        float Ka = 1;
        float Kd = .5;
        float Ks = .5;
        float roughness = .1;
        color specularcolor = 1;)
{

    /*Initialisation*/
    normal Nf = faceforward (normalize(N),I);
    vector V = -normalize(I);
    color Ct;

    /*Texturing*/
    Ct=Cs;

    /*Shading*/
    Oi = Os;
    Ci = Oi * ( Ct * (Ka*ambient() + Kd*diffuse(Nf)) +
        specularcolor * Ks*specular(Nf,V,roughness));
}
```

This is functionally identical to plastic, but it has now been broken into three sections: initialization, where V and Nf are set up; texturing, where we calculate a new variable Ct – the colour of the textured surface; and shading, where Ct is used in the plastic shading model. In our standard shader the textured surface colour Ct is simply assigned the value of Cs, but it is this texturing part of the shader we will be developing further.

We generally won't specify the whole shader in future, but simply the texturing section, as the shading and setup sections won't be changing in most of our examples. When a code fragment results in the calculation of Ct, it will be assumed that the code should be placed into the standard shader.

A simple ramp

Perhaps the simplest texture we could have is a ramp, where the texture changes colour smoothly across the surface. To do this you need to know where on the surface you currently are, and this information is provided by two variables, u and v, which tell us how far across and how far up (respectively) we are on the surface. Both range from 0 at the bottom left to 1 at the top right. This works for most of the RenderMan geometry types because they're based on patches – that is, they have four corners.

Although a sphere may not appear to have corners, you can unwrap the surface like a world map, u being longitude and v being latitude. Each point in the world can uniquely be identified by a set of two-dimensional coordinates. We can therefore take an image and wrap it onto a sphere to create a globe in a clear, simple fashion. This technique also works for all the other quadrics and all the patches (including NURBS).

Unfortunately such a neat mapping from u/v to a position of the object is not possible in the case of polygons, and this is one of the reasons their use is discouraged. Polygons do have u/v coordinates but they generally don't work very well. However, as the techniques required to get round this problem are a little more complex, we'll defer the subject for a later section.

You could use the variables u and v to calculate a value for Ct, but there's a slightly better way. RenderMan provides a second set of two-dimensional coordinates s and t, which by default are identical to u and v. These can be modified by the modeller, however, if the end user wishes to change the position of the texture. While u and v always refer to the underlying geometry, s and t refer to how the user wishes the surface to be textured. Generally you should use s and t to identify a position on a surface, and if the user doesn't change them then we're back to u,v anyway.

The texturing section of a simple ramp shader could therefore be as simple as Ct = s; which creates a ramp from black on the left to white on the right (Figure 20.1). Alternatively, Ct = t; creates the vertical ramp shown in Figure 20.2. For clarity these have been rendered on a simple tile which makes the texture coordinates most obvious.

Figure 20.1 A horizontal ramp.

Figure 20.2 A vertical ramp.

If you are from a programming background you might notice that something strange is going on. S is a scaler, that is, it contains a single value, which in this case ranges from 0 at the left, to 1 on the right, yet Ct is a colour which typically requires three components to specify the red, green and blue intensities. Most programming languages would consider assigning a float to an array to be an error of some sort, but SL is designed specifically to handle this sort of situation. SL knows that Ct is a colour, but it also knows that a float such as s can represent a grayscale value – an intensity. Assigning s to Ct therefore converts the grayscale value of 0 to black, 1 to white and similarly for shades of gray in between, hence we get the desired ramp.

A coloured ramp

If you wanted to convert the grayscale ramp into a colour ramp you would need to multiply the intensity s by a colour, and since the user has provided us with Cs it is probably best to use that (though we're under no obligation!). To produce a horizontal ramp we simply assign Ct=s*Cs. A similar vertical ramp could be generated using t*Cs.

The ramp of colour blends from black on the left to Cs on the right. To make the ramp to go the other way (from right to left) you could replace s with 1 - s. This places the most intense colour where s = 0 so 1 - s = 1 and black where s = 1 so 1 - s = 0.

A two-colour blend

By using different colours for the left–right and the right–left ramp then adding them together, you could produce a blend between the two – pure colour at each edge and then as one fades out the other would fade in. As this requires two colours we will specify the second with an expression: color "rgb" (0,1,0); which specifies bright green.

Note that in addition to providing the three component values of the colour, we have specified that these should be treated as an rgb value. Other colour spaces can be used to good effect, as in Plate II (The HSV colour space). The code in Listing 20.2 produces this image by simply using s to specify the hue, and t to specify the saturation.

Listing 20.2 The HSV colour space.

```
Ct=color "hsv" (s,t,1);
```

Having chosen the two colours to use we simply create a left–right ramp of green, a right–left ramp of the Cs, and add them together, as in Listing 20.3. However this mixing operation is so common that a standard function is provided to do it. mix() takes two colours and blends them together based upon the third float parameter, as demonstrated in Listing 20.4. The results of the two shaders, shown in Plate II (Blending two colours) are identical, though the code of Listing 20.4 is slightly clearer.

Listing 20.3 A colour blend.

```
color green;

green=color "rgb" (0,1,0);
Ct=(1-s)*Cs+s*green;
```

Listing 20.4 Using mix.

```
color green;

green=color "rgb" (0,1,0);
Ct=mix(Cs,green,s);
```

Generalizing the shader

Having arrived at an effect that we're happy with, the time comes to release the shader into general use. Before we do so, however, we should consider if we could make it a little more flexible. During development it made perfect sense to produce a green ramp from left to right, but once in use it would be frustrating to have to keep modifying the shader or maintain multiple copies each almost identical.

The most obvious limitation of the shader is that the user may want to choose their own colour. We should therefore probably replace the variable green with a parameter. Typically you should examine your shader for any constants that may need to be changed, and make these into parameters. However, you should also beware of making the shader too flexible – it is far simpler to have a number of shaders each creating one type of surface, than to have an incredibly complex shader with hundreds of parameters.

We might also choose to allow the user to select between a horizontal or vertical ramp. The completed shader including the standard template is shown in Listing 20.5.

Listing 20.5 A general ramp.

```
surface ramp (
    color otherColor=color "rgb" (0,1,0);
    float orientation=0;
    float Ka = 1;
    float Kd = .5;
    float Ks = .5;
    float roughness = .1;
    color specularcolor = 1;)
{
    normal Nf = faceforward (normalize(N),I);
    vector V = -normalize(I);
    color Ct;

    if(orientation==0)
        Ct=mix(Cs,otherColor,s);
    else
        Ct=mix(Cs,otherColor,t);

    Oi = Os;
    Ci = Oi * ( Ct * (Ka*ambient() + Kd*diffuse(Nf)) +
        specularcolor * Ks*specular(Nf,V,roughness));
}
```

Suggested activities

Attach ramp shaders to a range of geometric primitives and see how they behave. Which direction is s and which is t for each type of object? Try attaching texture coordinates in your modelling package. Use these to orient and control the ramp shaders.

Remember that though the standard shader template only varies the colour, you could use ramps to modify any part of the shading code. Try creating an `Ot` to modify the opacity, or an `Rt` to modify the surface roughness.

Summary

```
u,v - surface coordinates.
s,t - texture coordinates.
col=color "rgb" (r,g,b);
col=color "hsv" (h,s,v);
newcol=mix(col1, col2, blendval);
```

Chapter 21

Simple Patterns

Introduction

Having learnt that s and t can be used to specify points on
the surface of objects, we will now look at how we can use
these coordinates to draw patterns upon the surface. While
these shapes are quite simple, we can combine them together
with more complex results.

Bands

Perhaps the simplest pattern you could draw on a surface is
to divide it into two regions based on one of the texture
coordinates. To make the top red, and the bottom green as in
Plate IIIa you could use an if statement, and assign the chosen
colours to Ct appropriately. The code to do this is in Listing
21.1.

Listing 21.1 Creating bands.

```
color red=color "rgb" (1,0,0);
color green=color "rgb" (0,1,0);
if(t<0.5)
    Ct=green;
else
    Ct=red;
```

While this works, it creates a very sharp transition – a point
is either completely red or completely green. In a single still
frame this is not a problem, but in an animation pixels would
"pop" from one side to the other. This is just one instance of
a more general problem known is aliasing, which will be
discussed in greater depth in a later chapter. As a general rule
if statements should be used with caution in shaders.

To avoid such a sharp edge the transition from top to bottom
needs to be smoothed so that points on the border are
somewhere between red and green. This is done using the
function smoothstep(), which is plotted in Figure 21.1.
Smoothstep takes two parameters that represent the start

and the end of a transition, while a third parameter represents the position we're testing.

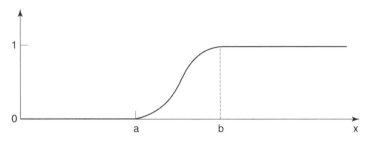

Figure 21.1 Smoothstep (a, b, x).

A revised shader based on smoothstep is shown in Listing 21.2. If t is less than 0.4 then the result will be 0, while inTop will be assigned 1 if t is greater than 0.6. Between these values the value returned by smoothstep will change gradually, avoiding any sharp transitions such as those produced by a conditional. The value inTop is then used to mix between red and green, to produce a soft edge, which avoids popping, as in Plate IIIb.

Listing 21.2 A soft edge.

```
float inTop;
color red=color "rgb" (1,0,0);
color green=color "rgb" (0,1,0);

inTop=smoothstep(0.4,0.6,t);

Ct=mix(green,red,inTop);
```

We can consider this kind of code as a sort of fuzzy logic. As in regular logic 1 means true – the point is in the top region – while 0 means false – that the point is not in the top. Some points are somewhere in between, however, so the variable inTop can also hold values somewhere between true and false.

Lines

If you need to produce a line vertically down the centre of the object you would first need to find the distance of the point being shaded from the centre:

```
float dist = abs (s-0.5);
```

We use the function abs() to throw away the sign of the result, as we don't care which side of the line the point is on.

If you wanted the line to be 0.2 wide then if dist is less than 0.1 we are considering a point in the line. Once again you should use smoothstep to soften the lines edge, as in Listing 21.3. We've used a variable fuzz to specify the softness of the edge, rather than adjusting the boundaries explicitly. We use 1-smoothstep() so that the result is 1 (true) inside the line, and zero (false) outside the line. The variable inLine is finally used to mix between red and green to produce the green line on a red background seen in Plate IIIc.

Listing 21.3 A vertical line.

```
color red=color "rgb" (1,0,0);
    color green=color "rgb" (0,1,0);
    float fuzz=0.025;

    float dist=abs(s-0.5);
    float inLine=1-smoothstep(0.1-fuzz,0.1+fuzz,dist);

    Ct=mix(red,green,inLine);
```

We could combine this line with the previous top/bottom split example to produce a blue line on a red and green background, seen in Plate IIId, by mixing the blue line over the old background which has been stored in Ct (Listing 21.4). This kind of layering allows patterns of greater complexity to be built up gradually from simple elements.

Listing 21.4 Layering two effects.

```
color red=color "rgb" (1,0,0);
color green=color "rgb" (0,1,0);
color blue=color "rgb" (0,0,1);
float fuzz=0.025;
float inTop;
float inLine;
float dist;

Ct=green;
inTop=smoothstep(0.5-fuzz,0.5+fuzz,t);
Ct=mix(Ct,red,inTop);

dist=abs(s-0.5);
inLine=1-smoothstep(0.1-fuzz,0.1+fuzz,dist);
Ct=mix(Ct,blue,inLine);
```

Circles

We can use the same approach to create a disk of colour, like Plate IIIe. We need to find the distance from the centre of the disk, and then decide if the point being shaded is inside or outside the shape. If we centre the disk at 0.5,0.5 then using Pythagoras, the distance from the centre to the current point is:

```
float dist = sqrt((s-0.5) * (s-0.5) + (t-0.5) *
(t-0.5));
```

We can simply drop this into our previous code, testing this distance to see if we are inside the disk, and then using the result to layer a new colour over the existing value of Ct, as in Listing 21.5. For increased flexibility we've set the background colour to Cs – as specified by the modeller.

Listing 21.5 A disk.

```
color blue=color "rgb" (0,0,1);
float fuzz=0.025;
float dist;
float inDisk;

Ct=Cs;

dist=sqrt((s-0.5)*(s-0.5)+(t-0.5)*(t-0.5));
inDisk=1-smoothstep(0.3-fuzz,0.3+fuzz,dist);
Ct=mix(Ct,blue,inDisk);
```

As an alternative to calculating the distance ourselves we could use the standard function distance(). This calculates the distance between two points in three dimensions. The only complication is that we need to turn our 2D texture coordinates into 3D points before we can pass them to distance. This is done as shown in Listing 21.6. Though it may appear as if we are calling a function called "point", it is in fact more analogous to a cast in C or perhaps a C++ constructor, which makes a point variable from three floating point coordinates.

The results from either approach are identical, and it is personal preference as to which one is clearer.

Listing 21.6 Using the distance function.

```
color blue=color "rgb" (0,0,1);
float fuzz=0.025;
float dist;
float inDisk;
point centre=point (0.5,0.5,0);
point here=point (s,t,0);

Ct=Cs;

dist=distance(centre,here);
inDisk=1-smoothstep(0.3-fuzz,0.3+fuzz,dist);
Ct=mix(Ct,blue,inDisk);
```

More lines

The lines we've drawn so far have been limited to being vertical or horizontal. To define arbitrary lines as in Plate IIIf you need to specify a start and an end point. The maths to calculate the distance of a point from a line is slightly more complex, but fortunately it is handled for us by the built-in function `ptlined()`. Given a start point, an end point, and the point to consider, it will return the required distance which we can then use in the standard fashion (Listing 21.7).

Listing 21.7 Using the `ptlined` function.

```
color blue=color "rgb" (0,0,1);
float fuzz=0.025;
float dist;
float inLine;
point start=point (0.1,0.3,0);
point end=point (0.7,0.7,0);
point here=point(s,t,0);

Ct=Cs;

dist=ptlined(start,end,here);
inLine=1-smoothstep(0.1-fuzz,0.1+fuzz,dist);
Ct=mix(Ct,blue,inLine);
```

Suggested activities

Use the techniques and functions you have learnt to draw some simple patterns. Use layers to build up more complex designs from simpler parts. What happens if you multiply `inDisk` by `inTop`, or (`1-inDisk`) by `inTop`? Could you use this approach to draw a rectangle?

Summary

```
float smoothstep(float start,
                 float end,
                 float here);
float mix(color c1, color c2, float blend);
float distance(point,point);
float ptlined(point start,
              point end,
              point here);
```

Chapter 22

Tiling and Repeating Patterns

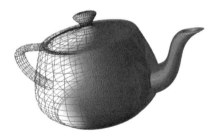

Introduction

In this chapter we will see how simple patterns can be duplicated across a surface to create a more complex pattern. We will use pseudo random numbers to modify the pattern upon each repeat to add visual interest to the texture.

Creating tiles

As all our patterns are based on the texture coordinates (s,t) we can manipulate these prior to the generation of the basic motif to produce a more complex overall effect. If the texture coordinates repeat, so will the pattern. The standard texture coordinates s and t cannot be changed, so we'll use two new variables, ss and tt to store these modified coordinates.

To duplicate a pattern horizontally five times we simply multiply s by five, then throw away the whole number part. This creates a new texture coordinate that goes from zero to one five times rather than once (Figure 22.1). We remove the integer part of a number using the mod() function which divides the first number by the second and returns the remainder. For example, mod(3.7,1) divides 3.7 by 1 which goes three times with 0.7 left over.

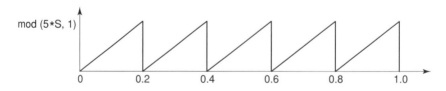

Figure 22.1 ss=mod(s*5,1);.

The modified texture coordinates are stored in ss (and tt) and then simply used to replace s and t throughout the rest of the texture. In Listing 22.1 we've used ss and tt in place of s and t in the disk texture from the previous chapter. The result, shown in Figure 22.2, is a repeating pattern over the surface:

Listing 22.1 A repeating pattern.

```
color blue=color "rgb" (0,0,1);
float fuzz=0.025;
float dist;
float inDisk;
float ss=mod(s*5,1);
float tt=mod(t*5,1);
point centre=point (0.5,0.5,0);
point here=point (ss,tt,0);

Ct=Cs;

dist=distance(centre,here);
inDisk=1-smoothstep(0.3-fuzz,0.3+fuzz,dist);
Ct=mix(Ct,blue,inDisk);
```

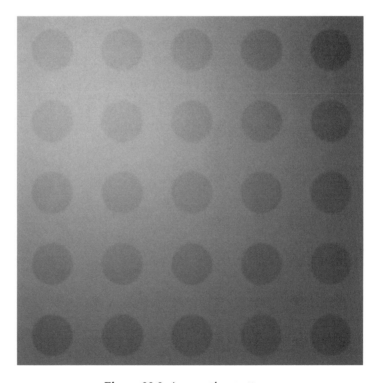

Figure 22.2 A repeating pattern.

Identifying tiles

To make this pattern more interesting we probably want to modify the basic motif so that it is slightly different in each cell. To do this you need to know which cell we're in as well as the out position in the cell. Where we used the mod() function to obtain the fractional part of a number we can use floor() to obtain the integer part, as in Listing 22.2. Here we've multiplied s by five, and then taken the integer part to obtain five distinct regions. We can then use the variable whichstripe to modify the surface. However, as this is constant over each region it will create stripes within the texture. In this case odd stripes are coloured white while even stripes are black.

Listing 22.2 Creating stripes.

```
float repeatCount=5;
float whichStripe=floor(s*repeatCount);
Ct=mod(whichStripe,2);
```

Figure 22.3 Creating stripes.

By applying this idea to both the s and t directions you can create a set of tiles where each tile is modified depending upon its position on the surface. We've done this in Listing 22.3. By simply adding together the stile and ttile values we create the checkerboard seen in Figure 22.4. Where the sum is odd we generate a white square, while even means a black square.

Listing 22.3 Creating tiles.

```
float repeatCount=5;
float sTile=floor(s*repeatCount);
float tTile=floor(t*repeatCount);
Ct=mod(sTile+tTile,2);
```

Figure 22.4 Creating tiles.

Though this does work it has the kind of sharp edges that you should use smoothstep to avoid and will look very bad when viewed from too far a way. We'll construct a better checkerboard in a later chapter, when we look at the problem of aliasing in greater detail.

CellNoise

Having established which tile we are shading, the next step is to generate a random value for that cell. We do not want the result to be truly random, however. In fact we want it to be consistent for the entire cell. This is the purpose of the cellnoise function. This takes a float, throws away the fractional part to obtain the tile number and then returns the result of a pseudo random calculation based upon that value. The important thing about this operation is that it will consistently return the same value for the whole cell. Listing 22.4 uses cellnoise to generate the random coloured stripes seen in Figure 22.5.

Listing 22.4 Random coloured stripes.

```
float repeatCount=5;
float ss=s*repeatCount;
Ct=color cellnoise(ss);
```

If you wanted to allocate colours in a grid, to create a randomly coloured set of tiles like Figure 22.6, then we could pass values based on both s and t coordinates to cellnoise. This is demonstrated in Listing 22.5.

Figure 22.5 *Random coloured stripes.*

Listing 22.5 Random coloured tiles.

```
float repeatCount=5;
float ss=s*repeatCount;
float tt=t*repeatCount;
Ct=color cellnoise(ss,tt);
```

Like many functions in SL cellnoise can take a varying number of parameters (one float, two floats, one point, or a point and a float). RenderMan will automatically use the right version. Even more flexibly cellnoise can generate either a single float (between 0 and 1), a colour or a vector of some kind. While RenderMan may be able to guess what kind of value it is expected to return, there is a good chance it may guess incorrectly, so you should always give RenderMan a hint by prefixing cellnoise with the required type.

Figure 22.6 *Random coloured tiles.*

In Listing 22.6 we use `cellnoise` to generate both a random colour and a random radius for a tiled set of disk. The radius of each disk is generated by a `float cellnoise()` function. As this normally returns a value of between 0 and 1 we've scaled it by 0.4 to ensure the disk fits within the cell. The result (Figure 22.7) is a texture that never repeats, and could easily be used on a large number of objects, and yet have each object appear different.

Listing 22.6 Random disks.

```
surface random (
        float Ka = 1;
        float Kd = .5;
        float Ks = .5;
        float roughness = .1;
        color specularcolor = 1;)
{
    normal Nf = faceforward (normalize(N),I);
    vector V = -normalize(I);
    color Ct;

    float fuzz=0.025;
    float repeatCount=5;
    float ss=mod(repeatCount*s,1);
    float tt=mod(repeatCount*t,1);
    point centre=point (0.5,0.5,0);
    point here=point (ss,tt,0);
    float dist=distance(centre,here);
    float radius=float cellnoise(repeatCount*s,
                              repeatCount*t)*0.4;
    color myColor=color cellnoise(repeatCount*s,
                              repeatCount*t);
    float inDisk=1-smoothstep(radius-fuzz,
                              radius+fuzz,dist);
    Ct=mix(Cs,myColor,inDisk);


    Oi = Os;
    Ci = Oi * ( Ct * (Ka*ambient() + Kd*diffuse(Nf)) +
        specularcolor * Ks*specular(Nf,V,roughness));
}
```

Figure 22.7 Random disks.

Other modifications to ss and tt

Though tiling is very common in shaders it is certainly not the only way you can modify the texture coordinates. ss and tt can be generated in any fashion to scale, rotate or distort the basic pattern. For example, in Listing 22.7 we've added a sine wave to the s coordinate, before using the result in texture that would normally produce a vertical line. By using the deformed texture coordinates we get the wavy line in Figure 22.8 which is visually far more interesting.

Listing 22.7 Deforming the texture coordinates.

```
color green=color "rgb" (0,1,0);
float fuzz=0.025;
```

```
float ss=s+sin(t*2*PI)*0.4;

float dist=abs(ss-0.5);
float inLine=1-smoothstep(0.1-fuzz,0.1+fuzz,dist);
Ct=mix(Cs,green,inLine);
```

Figure 22.8 *Deforming the texture coordinates.*

Suggested activities

Look around you for repeating patterns like bricks, wallpaper, planks or paving stones. How might you generate tiles which repeat in these patterns?

Take the shaders you've written to generate simple patterns, and modify them so they tile the surface. Add some randomization so that each repeat is slightly different.

Consider adding parameters to allow the user to control both the repeating and variation.

Of course there's no reason why every layer of your texture should be tiled the same way. ss and tt could be generated several times in a single shader using different values of repeatCount.

Summary

```
ss=mod(s*numberOfTiles,1);
whichTileS=floor(s*numberOfTiles);
x=float cellnoise(s);
x=float cellnoise(s,t);
Ct=color cellnoise(s);
Ct=color cellnoise(s,t);
```

Chapter 23

Projections and Coordinate Spaces

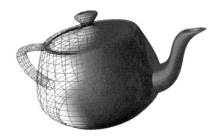

Introduction

In this chapter we will see how you can use the position of points in 3D space to texture surfaces. This allows you to create objects that appear to be carved from blocks, and to texture objects for which texture coordinates are inadequate.

3D coordinates

While s and t are simple and convenient, it is not always possible or appropriate to use them. While patches have well-defined surface coordinates, other forms of geometry such as polygons, subdivision surfaces and blobby objects cannot be mapped so easily. Even when patches are being used it can be difficult to create seamless textures when an object is constructed from more than one patch. In these cases we need to find other ways of identifying where we are in the texture.

Regardless of the type of surface, you can always identify each point to be shaded by its position in 3D space. This is stored in the global variable P. It is therefore always possible to base the surface colour calculation upon this value. You could, for example, simply take the x and y positions, and use those as the basis of our texturing as in Listing and Figure 23.1. This is an orthographic projection, as the texture is projected along the z axis. The components of a point (or vector) are extracted using the functions xcomp, ycomp and zcomp. In this case we've simply used the new texture coordinates, ss and tt, as parameters to cellnoise which allows us to see how the texture wraps around the object. However, you could use these coordinates as the basis for any of the effects so far explored.

Listing 23.1 Orthographic projection.

```
float repeatCount=5;
float ss=xcomp(P)*repeatCount;
float tt=ycomp(P)*repeatCount;
Ct=color cellnoise(ss,tt);
```

Figure 23.1 *Orthographic projection.*

Coordinate systems

Though P specifies a point in 3D space it is undefined *which* space it is in. If we are shading a sphere we might reasonably like to consider P as being relative to the centre of the sphere. However, transformations are applied to each object to position it relative to the rest of the objects in the world. The world itself is defined relative to the camera's position. P might define the point we are shading relative to the object it is part of, relative to the world, relative to the camera, or relative to some totally different frame of reference.

In fact P is defined as being in "current" space – a coordinate system selected by the renderer that is undefined by the RenderMan standard. In a ray tracer this is usually equivalent to "object": the coordinate system in which the object was created, while a scanline renderer would typically use "camera": a coordinate system where the camera is at the origin, and pointing down the z axis.

Figure 23.1 was created in a renderer in which "current" space is equivalent to "camera", but given that "current" space is renderer dependent it is clearly foolish to rely on it when applying textures. A different renderer might produce a very different image. Rather than relying on the renderer's choice of coordinate system, you should always transform the point P into a specific frame of reference.

In Listing 23.2 we've created a similar shader to the one used previously, but this time we've specified that the calculations should be done relative to the position of the object. This is done by transforming the position of P into object space, and assigning it to the new variable PP which is used for the rest of the calculation. Again we've used a convention of PP being some modified version of the variable P.

Listing 23.2 Object space.

```
point PP=transform("object",P);

float repeatCount=5;
float ss=xcomp(PP)*repeatCount;
float tt=ycomp(PP)*repeatCount;

Ct=color cellnoise(ss,tt);
```

When this new shader is applied to the scene we previously shaded in current space we get the image in Figure 23.2. The spheres are shaded relative to the coordinate system in which they were created, rather than the position in which they occupy relative to the camera. You can now see that the sphere on the right is in fact rotated, as the squares of colour run through it from top to bottom rather than front to back.

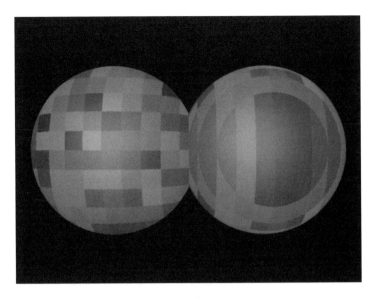

Figure 23.2 Object space.

If you use "object" space to define the coordinates in a shader, then the texture will move as the object does, while if "world" is used the object will swim through the texture. Between these two spaces is "shader" space – the coordinate space in which the shader is specified, which we've used in Listing 23.3.

Listing 23.3 Shader space.

```
point PP=transform("shader",P);

float repeatCount=5;
float ss=xcomp(PP)*repeatCount;
float tt=ycomp(PP)*repeatCount;

Ct=color cellnoise(ss,tt);
```

By applying a shader to a group of several objects, they will share their "shader" coordinate system as seen in Figure 23.3. Here the shader has been created in a rotated coordinate space, and hence the texture appears to be rotated. By texturing in shader space the separate objects will be textured as a single object, allowing you to easily create textures which flow smoothly from one primitive to the next.

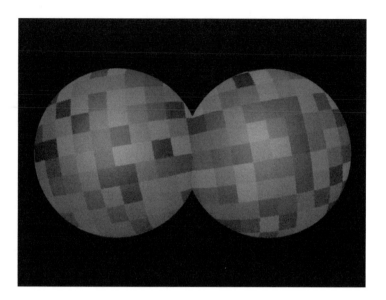

Figure 23.3 Shader space.

It is also possible to shade in "camera" space, which gives the position of the object relative to the camera. Using this would cause objects to change their appearance as the camera moves which would generally be undesirable, but you could use it to create "intelligent" surfaces which change as you look at them.

More complex projections

When painted or photographed textures are used you often need to project them as if from a single point, rather like a slide projector. This is a perspective transformation, and is achieved by dividing the x and y values by the z depth as in Listing 23.4. This particular shader projects a texture from the camera rather like a traditional front projection system. This matches the way the camera projects back onto the film, and hence the result shown in Figure 23.4 is a different effect to that seen in 23.1, which used an orthographic projection in camera space.

Listing 23.4 Perspective projection.

```
point PP=transform("camera",P);

float repeatCount=20;
float ss=xcomp(PP)/zcomp(PP)*repeatCount;
float tt=ycomp(PP)/zcomp(PP)*repeatCount;

Ct=color cellnoise(ss,tt);
```

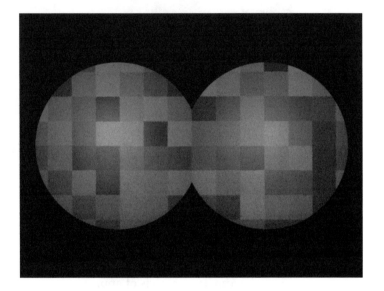

Figure 23.4 *Perspective projection.*

For certain types of shape (such as the heads on characters), the most appropriate projection is a cylindrical one. This takes the *z* coordinate as the t component, and the angle around the axis as the s component. It can be calculated by the code in Listing 23.5. The resulting image in Figure 23.5 is textured as if you'd wrapped the texture into a cylinder, and then shrink-wrapped it onto the object.

Listing 23.5 Cylindrical projection.

```
point PP=transform("object",P);

float repeatCount=10;
```

```
float ss=atan(xcomp(PP),zcomp(PP))/(2*PI)*repeatCount;
float tt=ycomp(PP)*repeatCount;

Ct=color cellnoise(ss,tt);
```

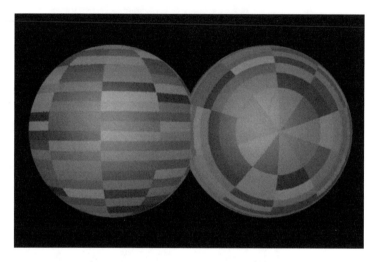

Figure 23.5 *Cylindrical projection.*

The other common projection type is spherical, as in Listing 23.6. This textures the object in a similar fashion to the standard st coordinates of a sphere, but may be used for any kind of geometry which is of approximately spherical shape. While ss is identical to cylindrical, the tt coordinates are mapped differently. This is particularly noticeable at the top of the objects, as seen in the right-hand sphere of Figure 23.6, and so you might use it in preference to cylindrical if you needed to look down at the top of a character's head.

Listing 23.6 Spherical projection.

```
float repeatCount=10;
float ss,tt;
vector PP=transform("object",P);
PP=normalize(PP);

ss=(atan(xcomp(PP),zcomp(PP))/(2*PI))*repeatCount;
tt=acos(ycomp(PP))/PI*repeatCount;
Ct=color cellnoise(ss,tt);;
```

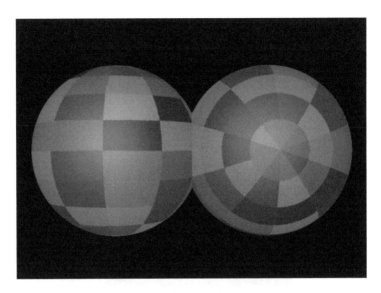

Figure 23.6 Spherical projection.

Solid textures

Rather than projecting the point P into two dimensions, and using the 2D coordinates as the basis for texturing, you could skip that stage completely, and use the value of P directly to construct a texture. This creates a texture that changes smoothly regardless of how the surface is shaped, and produces an object that appears to have been carved from a solid block of the material. For this reason such textures are generally referred to as solid textures. Extending our tiling examples to three dimensions, you can carve the spheres from cubes of colour as in Listing 23.7 and Figure 23.7.

Listing 23.7 Spheres carved from cubes.

```
point PP=transform("object",P);

float repeatCount=5;

Ct=color cellnoise(PP*repeatCount);
```

Figure 23.7 Spheres carved from cubes.

Solid textures avoid the appearance that a pattern has simply been pasted onto the surface of an object, but rather that it is a real part of the object. We'll see how this can create wood and marble effects in a later chapter.

More coordinate system transforms

We have so far assumed that you're transforming a point from the default "current" space to a new coordinate system. However, you might need to transform from this new coordinate system to a third. This can be done by passing both "from" and "to" coordinate systems to the transform command. For example:

```
point origin=transform("camera",
                       "object",
                       point (0,0,0));
```

calculates the position of the camera in object space, by transforming the point 0,0,0 from camera space to object space.

You should take care as to exactly what kind of vector we are transforming. So far, only points have been transformed, but surface normals and free vectors may also be transformed between coordinate systems. Different types of vector need to be changed in different ways when converted. Transform() is designed to transform points. To make sure that you get the correct type of conversion you should use the functions vtransform() and ntransform() when converting vectors, and surface normals respectively.

Suggested activities

Modify some of your shaders to use projections from 3D space. Consider which coordinate system is appropriate for a range of applications. Consider adding a parameter:

```
string space = "shader";
```

to your shaders, allowing the user to choose an appropriate coordinate system.

Experiment with functions like distance() and ptlined() to see how they behave in 3D space.

Summary

```
point transform([fromspace],tospace,P);
vector vtransform([fromspace],tospace,V);
normal ntransform([fromspace],tospace,N);
```
Coordinate Spaces;
"object"
"shader"
"world"
"camera"

Related functions

It is also possible to create new named coordinate systems using the RIB command CoordinateSystem "name". This allows textures to be easily projected onto a surface from any position required.

Chapter 24

Painted Textures

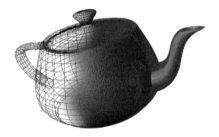

Introduction

Though writing code is a powerful way of texturing objects, sometimes it is simply easier to paint something by hand then apply that to the object. We're going to see how that can be done in RenderMan, but more importantly we'll look at how painted textures can be combined with procedural textures to give the user the maximum power and control.

Accessing texture maps

Some patterns can be constructed easily using SL code, but for other types of pattern it is clearly easier to paint or photograph the required design, then apply this image to the three-dimensional object. Even in these cases, however, a shader is still required: first to calculate which point on the source image (known as a texture map) corresponds to the surface point being calculated, and then to define how the value from the map will affect the surface.

The most obvious and simplest use of a texture would be to take Ct from the map using the default texture coordinates (s and t). You can do this simply by using the code in Listing 24.1. The renderer does all the hard work for you, taking into account the file format, and resolution, resizing it automatically to fit the object, to produce an image like Figure 24.1.

Listing 24.1 Accessing a texture.

```
Ct=color texture("myTexture.tiff");
```

Figure 24.1 *Accessing a texture.*

Generally, the texture map will be provided by the user of the shader when it is applied in a scene. You should therefore make the name of the map a parameter of the shader, so that it can be specified at render time. In such cases, the shader usually contains code similar to Listing 24.2, which first checks that a file name has been provided, so that if the user chooses not to provide a map, the shader will still operate correctly. In order to simplify the examples in this chapter, however, we will continue to hard code the file names.

Listing 24.2 An optional texture map.

```
surface param (
        ...
        string mapname= "";
        ...)
```

```
{
...

if(mapname != "")
            Ct=color texture(mapname);
else
            Ct=Cs;

...
}
```

Procedurally modifying a texture map

The texture function automatically wraps the texture onto the surface using s and t. As you've learnt, however, simple patterns can be augmented by modifying the texture coordinates before you generate a pattern. In exactly the same way we can calculate new texture coordinate, and ask texture() to use these to position the map on the object. In Listing 24.3 we've combined the texture lookup with some standard tiling code to cover the object with copies of the image as shown in Figure 24.2. Combining SL with a texture map gives you total control over texture placement, as you can use any function to generate the texture coordinates. For example in Listing 24.4 we've added a sine wave to ss, and hence deformed the image as in Figure 24.3.

Listing 24.3 Tiling a texture map.

```
float repeatCount=5;
float ss=mod(s*repeatCount,1);
float tt=mod(t*repeatCount,1);

Ct=color texture("pebbles.tiff",ss,tt);
```

Figure 24.2 Tiling a texture map.

Listing 24.4 Distorting a texture map.

```
float ss=mod(s*2+0.1*sin(t*10),1);
float tt=t;

Ct=color texture("pebbles.tiff",ss,tt);
```

Figure 24.3 *Distorting a texture map.*

You could even use `cellnoise` to randomly select between a number of images for each tile, as we've done in Listing 24.5. This combination of coded and painted textures allows you to avoid one of the primary problems of texture maps – that they are always the same. Here we've created a texture which can be applied to as large an area as we require yet will never repeat, as seen in Figure 24.4. Of course these textures do not tile together correctly, and hence the joins are very apparent, but by carefully repainting the texture maps, and perhaps a slightly more complex shader, the results could be convincing.

Listing 24.5 Mixing between texture maps.

```
float repeatCount=5;
float ss=mod(s*repeatCount,1);
float tt=mod(t*repeatCount,1);
```

```
if(float cellnoise(s*repeatCount,t*repeatCount)>0.5)
    Ct=color texture("pebbles.tiff",ss,tt);
else
    Ct=color texture("rock.tiff",ss,tt);
```

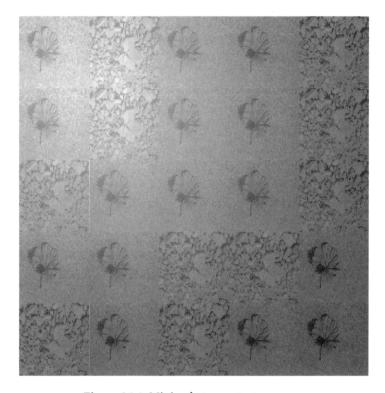

Figure 24.4 Mixing between texture maps.

Maps as controls for procedural textures

Rather than simply using a texture map as an image that is painted onto the surface and using code to control it, you can also use the painted map to control procedural elements of the shader. Suppose you wish to model a surface that has corroded in certain areas, and have by some mechanism created a rust texture. Rather than trying to provide parameters to the shader defining which areas are shiny and which are rust, you could use a texture map to let an artist paint the areas in which the rust colouring is used. In this case the texture isn't being used as a colour, but simply as a control. We use "float texture" rather than "color texture" to indicate we want a grayscale value (just as we did with cellnoise).

Such an example is shown in Listing 24.6. It assumes that we have already generated the rust variable, then uses the painted texture to decide where the rust is visible, and where the original surface colour should be used. It also uses the texture map to modify the weighting of specularity and diffuse lighting, so that the underlying surface is more metallic while the rust layer is almost matte. The resulting image is shown in Figure 24.5.

Listing 24.6 Using a map as a control.

```
float freq=20;
color rust=A_RUST_TEXTURE_WEVE_GENERATED;

float surfaceType=float texture("rust.tiff");
Ct=mix(Cs,rust,surfaceType);


Oi = Os;
Ci = Oi * ( Ct * (Ka*ambient() +
surfaceType*diffuse(Nf) +
    (1-surfaceType)*specular(Nf,V,roughness)));
```

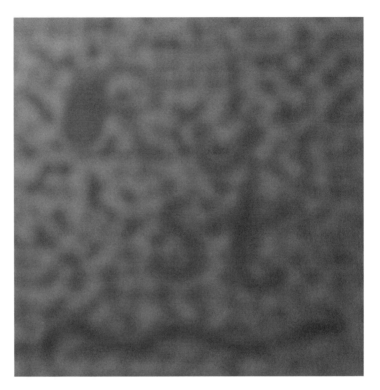

Figure 24.5 *Using a map as a control.*

Environment maps

Texture maps that are accessed by surface coordinates are the simplest and most common form of map, but 2D images may be applied to surfaces in other ways. If your renderer does not support ray tracing, or even if it does but it is too slow, then environment maps provide a flexible alternative. If you're trying to mix live action with CG, you can even use them to create reflections of real objects.

The basic assumption made when using environment maps is that you're rendering a small object in a big world. If we were ray tracing the object then a ray from the camera would hit a point on the object, and then a reflected ray would be traced back into the rest of the scene. However, if the object were very small and the environment very big it wouldn't matter which point on the surface of the object we were considering – we only need to worry about the direction of the reflected ray, as illustrated in Figure 24.6.

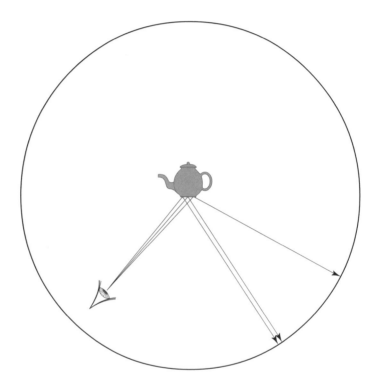

Figure 24.6 A small object in a big world.

If we were to photograph the scene from the centre of the object, and stitched the images together into a panoramic view, then you could extract the colour of the environment in any direction from the photograph. Such a photograph is an environment map.

Of course, it is only an approximation, as the point being rendered isn't actually at the centre of the object. Despite this, it is usually an approximation that is good enough to fool most of the people most of the time. As we only need to produce one map for the whole object, and perhaps only one map for a whole scene, if the environment is not changing significantly then this is potentially much more efficient than ray tracing.

Generating environment maps

When generated by rendering or from photographs, environment maps usually take the form of six square images, one each in the positive and negative *x*, *y* and *z* directions, forming the six faces of a cube around the object. Such a collection of image is usually displayed as in Figure 24.7. These are stitched together by the `MakeCube FaceEnvironment` RIB command. This takes the six input files followed by the name of the output file, and a field of view value for the input images. This should generally be a little over 90 degrees so that there are no gaps between the images. The final parameters describe how the image should be filtered: "`gaussian`" 2 2 are appropriate values.

Figure 24.7 *A cube face environment.*
(Courtesy of Jerome Dewhurst, www.photographica.co.uk)

While the cubic form is easy to render and photograph, it does have the disadvantage of not being a single image. This makes it hard for artists to work with in paint packages, and other image manipulation tools. You may prefer to use a polar form of environment map shown in Figure 24.8. This unwraps the texture from the surface of a sphere in exactly the same way as a world map could be unwrapped from a globe. Though the whole map is a single image it must still be converted to your renderer's proprietary format using the RIB command `MakeLongLatEnvironment`. Being simpler than the cubic form this simply requires an input file, an output file name, and a filter function(`"gaussian" 2 2`).

Figure 24.8 A polar environment map.
(Courtesy of Jerome Dewhurst, www.photographica.co.uk)

A stand-alone program to generate environment maps from either cubic or polar images may also have been supplied with your renderer.

Applying environment maps

Once converted to the renderer's internal format, we can forget how an environment was generated and instead concentrate upon using it in our shader. To do this we need to first calculate the direction of reflection, and then find the colour of the map in that direction.

While it is quite simple to calculate the direction of reflection from the position of the viewer and the orientation of the surface, RenderMan provides a function to do the work for us. By simply calling the reflect function as in Listing 24.7, the required direction is calculated. Note that reflect is simply a geometric calculation, and is not performing any kind of ray tracing.

Listing 24.7 A reflective surface.

```
surface reflect (
        float Ka = 1;
        float Kd = .5;
        float Ks = .4;
        float Kr = .3;
        float roughness = .1;
        color specularcolor = 1;)
{
    normal Nf = faceforward (normalize(N),I);
    vector V = -normalize(I);
    color Ct;
    vector Rcurrent=reflect(I,Nf);
    vector Rworld=vtransform("world",Rcurrent);
    color Cr=color environment("studio2.jpg",Rworld);

    Ct=Cs;

    Oi = Os;
    Ci = Oi * ( Ct * (Ka*ambient() + Kd*diffuse(Nf)) +
        specularcolor * (Ks*specular(Nf,V,roughness)+Kr*Cr));
}
```

Once you know the direction of reflection you simply have to pass this, along with the name of the map, to the environment function, and the correct value from the map is returned. However, be sure to convert the direction to an appropriate space, so that the environment map is correctly oriented onto the object. As the value from the environment map represents reflected light we've added it into the plastic shading model with the specular contribution.

The resulting reflections, as seen in Figure 24.9 (also Plate VI) are not physically accurate, but in many cases it will be close enough to fool all but the most critical viewer.

Figure 24.9 A reflective surface (also Plate VI).

Suggested activities

Investigate what formats of image files are supported by your renderer. You may need to convert your textures to some proprietary format in order to obtain optimum image quality and performance.

Examine the shaders you have written and consider if they would benefit from the inclusion of a texture map. Use maps to either place detailed artwork onto a surface, or control procedurally generated effects.

Select a shader you have written which creates a shiny surface and add an environment map. Try photographing, painting or rendering such a map, and apply it to your object.

Summary

```
float texture(filename,s,t);
color texture(filename,s,t);
vector R=reflect(I,N);
```

```
float environment(filename,R);
color environment(filename,R);
```

RIB commands

```
MakeCubeFaceEnvironment "px" "nx" "py" "ny" "pz"
"nz" "envmapname" fov "gaussian" 2 2
MakeLongLatEnvironment "srcmapname" "envmapname"
"gaussian" 2 2
```

Related functions

vector R=refract(I,N,eta)

Refract calculates the direction of refraction as reflect does for reflection. Eta is the ratio of the two refractive indices at the surface.

fresnel(I,N,eta,Kr,Kt,R,T)

Fresnel calculates both reflection and refraction directions (returned in R and T) along with suggested values as to how these should be weighted when mixed with the rest of the shading calculation (Kr and Kt).

color trace(location,direction)

Your renderer may support ray tracing, in which case, the function trace may be used in place of environment().

It is also possible to improve the perceived accuracy of environment maps by including P in the calculation of the reflection direction. This is discussed in *Advanced RenderMan.*

Chapter

25

Displacement

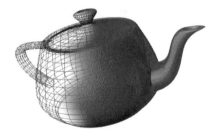

Introduction

Shaders can not only change the colour and lighting across a surface but can actually change the shape of the surface – a technique known as displacement. This allows you to produce simpler models then fill in surface detail at render time.

Modifying P

In addition to using P to calculate texture coordinates in a surface shader it is also possible (in most renderers) to modify P, and in doing so change the shape of the surface. For greater flexibility, and to ease implementation, changing the position of a point on the surface is done in a separate shader to the calculation of surface colour. This is known as a "displacement" shader, and is run before the surface shader: the renderer creates a smooth surface, runs the displacement shader to find its final position and orientation, then runs the surface shader to find its colour. This process is shown in Figure 25.1.

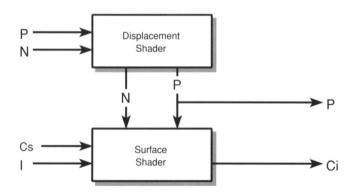

Figure 25.1 The displacement process.

Officially, the position of a surface should only be modified by a displacement shader but in practice most renderers also allow displacement to be performed in a surface shader. Displacing in a surface shader allows calculations to be performed once, and then used for both displacement and colouring (for example, embossing a coloured stripe on a surface), while a separate shader allows a displacement to be mixed with a variety of surface types. In practice, both approaches are used, though we'll use displacement shaders here, as this is the method that is officially supported.

While in principle it is possible to assign any value to P, displacement typically consists of moving the surface in or out a short distance along the surface normal. The displacement shader's job is therefore to calculate the magnitude of this displacement for each point. Most displacement shaders have a structure similar to Listing 25.1.

Listing 25.1 A simple displacement shader.

```
displacement simple (
    float Km = 0.1;)
{
    normal NN = normalize(N);
    float mag=0;

    /*Calculate mag*/
    mag=sin(s*10*2*PI)*sin(t*10*2*PI);

    /*Displace*/
    P=P+mag*Km*NN;
    N=calculatenormal(P);
}
```

The surface normal vector can have varying length, so it is first normalized, so its length does not affect the displacement. You can then insert some arbitrary calculation for mag – here we've used a combination of sine waves in s and t. Displacement is performed by adding some multiple of N to the current position, and assigning it back to the variable P. A parameter to the shader Km provides a control over the total amount of displacement. Having moved the points of the surface, its curvature will have changed and hence we recalculate the surface normals (N) by using the function `calculatenormal`. Though simple, the combination of shape and lighting produces a remarkably interesting pattern when applied to a sphere in Figure 25.2.

Figure 25.2 *A simple displacement shader.*

In the same way that we calculated `Ct` in the standard surface shader and then placed that code into a standard framework, for most displacement shaders you simply need to calculate `mag`. To arrive at a value for `mag`, you can apply any of the techniques you've learnt so far. For example, to emboss a circle onto the surface like Figure 25.3, you could use the same approach you previously used to draw a coloured circle, as in Listing 25.2.

Listing 25.2 Embossing a disk.

```
displacement disk (
    float Km = 0.1;)
{
    normal NN = normalize(N);
    float mag=0;
    float fuzz=0.05;
```

```
/*Calculate mag*/
float dist=sqrt((s-0.5)*(s-0.5)+(t-0.5)*(t-0.5));
mag=smoothstep(0.3-fuzz,0.3+fuzz,dist);

/*Displace*/
P=P+mag*Km*NN;
N=calculatenormal(P);
}
```

Figure 25.3 *Embossing a disk.*

Displacing in the right space

While this function will operate correctly, its exact behaviour is not consistent between different renderers. As we discussed previously, all shading is done in coordinate space known as "current" but the exact meaning of this space is left to the designer of the renderer to decide. While we know the value of N in current space, it is unclear what the length "mag" means in any particular space. If current were equivalent to object then the displacement would scale with the object, while if current were "camera" then scaling the object would leave the displacement unaffected. Figure 25.4 shows a sine wave pattern embossed onto two spheres – the second sphere being a scaled version of the first. Unfortunately because the displacement has been performed in current space the displacement is the same size in both cases, which is unlikely to be the effect you want.

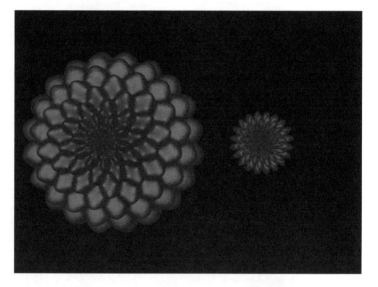

Figure 25.4 Displacing a current space.

While there is no correct space in which displacement distances should be specified, "object" or "shader" are probably most appropriate, and this can be implemented by including the line:

```
mag /= length(vtransform("object",NN));
```

This scales the displacement by the length of N in object space, and hence mag is now relative to that space. Figure 25.5

shows the effect of adding this to the previous code to produce the shader in Listing 25.3. The displacement has now been scaled, so the two objects correctly appear to be scaled versions of each other. Of course you may choose to displace in other spaces, such as shader or world. For maximum flexibility the displacement space can be specified by a parameter to the shader.

Listing 25.3 Displacing in object space.

```
displacement object (
    float Km = 0.1;)
{
    vector NN = normalize(N);
    float mag=0;

    /*Calculate mag*/
    mag=sin(s*10*2*PI)*sin(t*10*2*PI);
    mag /= length (vtransform("object",NN));

    /*Displace*/
    P=P+mag*Km*NN;
    N=calculatenormal(P);
}
```

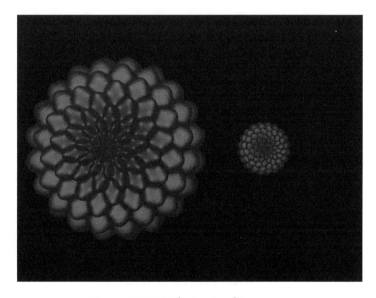

Figure 25.5 Displacing in object space.

Not moving P

As an alternative to actually moving the point, we may choose to simply re-orient that the point, so that it is lit as if it were displaced, but the points remain in their original position. This approach is called bumping, and while it may not always appear as convincing as true displacement it puts less strain on the rendering engine, and can avoid certain artifacts. It is also more likely to be supported, and is guaranteed to work correctly in surface shaders.

To bump a surface, simply calculate the new surface position, as if for displacement, but do not assign the position back to P. We then use this value, which is typically called PP to calculate the new surface normal.

A bumped version of the previous displacement is shown in Listing 25.4. When this is rendered in Figure 25.6 you can see that while bump mapping works well on the smaller object, it becomes obvious that something is wrong, as the sphere becomes larger.

Listing 25.4 A bump shader.

```
displacement simpleBump (
    float Km = 0.1;)
{
    vector NN = normalize(N);
    float mag=0;
    point PP;

    /*Calculate mag*/
    mag=sin(s*10*2*PI)*sin(t*10*2*PI);
    mag /= length(vtransform("object",NN));

    /*Displace*/
    PP=P+mag*Km*NN;
    N=calculatenormal(PP);
}
```

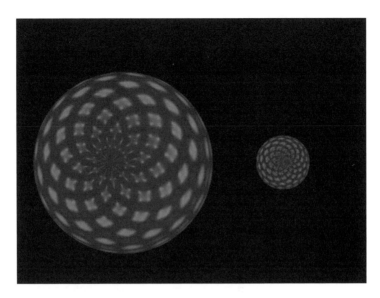

Figure 25.6 *A bump shader.*

As the processes of bumping and displacing are so similar, it is good practice to provide the user of a displacement shader with the option of either bumping or displacing. You can do this with a simple parameter, as shown in Listing 25.5. This shader incorporates all of the improvements we've made, and can be used as a standard template for displacement shaders.

Listing 25.5 A standard displacement shader.

```
displacement standardDisplace (
    float Km = 0.1;
    string space= "object";
    float trueDisp=1;)
{

    vector NN = normalize(N);
    float mag=0;
    point PP;

    /*Calculate mag*/
    mag=sin(s*10*2*PI)*sin(t*10*2*PI);
    mag /= length(vtransform(space,NN));
```

```
/*Displace*/
PP=P+mag*Km*NN;
N=calculatenormal(PP);

if(trueDisp==1)
    P=PP;
}
```

Suggested activities

Take code from the surface shaders you have written and try applying the patterns as displacements. Try using these displacement shaders with the original surface shaders so that the displacement and surface colour follow each other.

Verify that your renderer supports true displacement (or it may be an option you need to enable). Try each shader you develop as both a bump and a displacement. Decide which works best on a range of objects.

Try using texture maps in a displacement shader to "paint" extra detail into your models.

Summary

```
N = calculatenormal(point PP);
```

Chapter 26

Noise

Introduction

The patterns we've developed so far enable us to construct geometric designs on the surface of objects, but even the most carefully manufactured objects have imperfections. It is precisely these imperfections which give real world objects their sense of scale and physical presence. We'll now consider how you can use a shader to roughen a surface, avoiding the mathematically perfect appearance that instantly marks an image as computer generated.

Controlled randomness

To add visual interest to a surface we need to introduce some kind of randomness, but using a standard random function would be of little use. A normal random number would be totally different from frame to frame, and renders would simply not be repeatable. The `cellnoise` function is repeatable because it always returns the same value for each cell. This is only possible, however, because the cells are based on integers. Floating point values are susceptible to rounding errors, so that two values we might think are the same are probably minutely different, and hence a repeatable random number generator based on floating point values would be unreliable.

These problems are solved by a function known as `Noise`. This generates a value which can be used to provide randomness in our textures, but it changes smoothly. Small changes in the input produce small changes in the output, making it tolerant to rounding errors.

Noise

The `Noise` function in RenderMan can take a varying number of parameters, and return a range of types (much like `cellnoise`). The values returned are guaranteed to be between 0 and 1, and average 0.5. The value returned is also guaranteed to be 0.5 if the input is an integer, and will change smoothly between these "lattice points". Within these limitations, the exact values returned by `Noise` are unique to each renderer, but when used correctly, all renderers will produce similar images. A sample from a typical `Noise` function is shown in Figure 26.1.

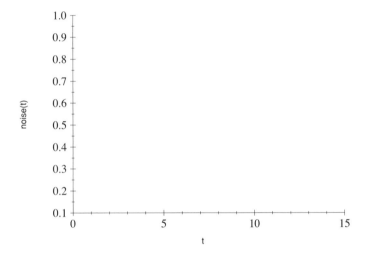

Figure 26.1 Noise.

You could assign a noise value to `Ct` as in Listing 26.1. This produces a gently changing brightness over the surface. However, by scaling the texture coordinates, as in Figure 26.2 you can produce noise at a range of frequencies. While noise is random at larger scales, it is smooth when viewed more closely. This allows you to use noise to add visual interest at various levels of detail.

Listing 26.1 Noise over a 2D surface.

```
float repeatCount=10;
Ct=float noise(s*repeatCount,t*repeatCount);
```

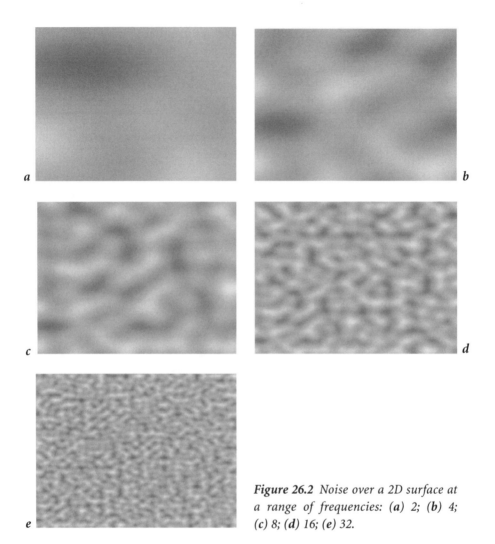

Figure 26.2 *Noise over a 2D surface at a range of frequencies: (a) 2; (b) 4; (c) 8; (d) 16; (e) 32.*

In Listing 26.2 we've based the noise value on P rather than s and t, resulting in a noise value which can be used as the basis of a solid texture (Figure 26.3). Note how the texture runs smoothly between the two spheres as if they were carved out of a single block of material. We've also used the "color" form of noise which returns a colour rather than a single floating point value.

Listing 26.2 "Solid" noise.

```
point PP=transform("shader",P);

Ct=color noise(PP*10);
```

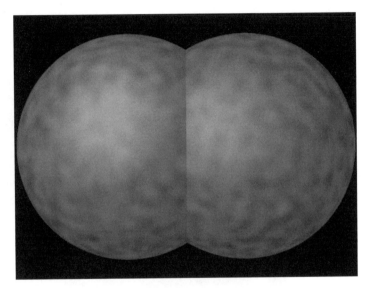

Figure 26.3 *"solid" noise.*

Distorting texture coordinates

Rather than assigning noise directly to a surface, or mixing it into another colour, you can also achieve useful results by using noise to distort the texture coordinates. This will break up the straight lines that are generated by simple pattern code. Figure 26.4 was created by the shader in Listing 26.3, which uses a Noise function of P to distort the surface coordinates so that the cellnoise function produces randomly shaped patches of colour, rather than squares. The offset of 100, which is added to P in the second noise call, is so that the distortion in t is different to the distortion in s. Any value could be used provided it is reasonably large.

Listing 26.3 Using noise to deform textures.

```
float ss=s+float noise(P*5)*0.5;
float tt=t+float noise(P*5+point(100,100,100))*0.5;

Ct=color cellnoise(ss*10,tt*10);
```

Figure 26.4 *Using noise to deform textures.*

This approach is incredibly powerful, as it prevents your surfaces from appearing too geometric. For example, it can be used to generate wood textures, by deforming a series of concentric cylinders representing tree rings, as shown in Listing 26.4 and Figure 26.5. As both the noise and cylinders are based upon the value of P rather than surface coordinates, this is a solid texture, giving the appearance that the teapot is made out of wood rather than simply having a wood veneer applied to its surface.

Listing 26.4 A wood texture.

```
point PP;
float l;
float scale=0.1;
```

```
/*Generate a distored P in shader space */
PP=ptransform("shader",P)*scale;
PP=PP+point noise(PP*10)*0.1;

/*Calculate radius*/
l=sqrt(xcomp(PP)*xcomp(PP)+ycomp(PP)*ycomp(PP));

/*mix between light and dark wood*/
Ct=mix(darkWood,lightWood,mod(l*8,1));
```

Figure 26.5 A wood texture.

fBm

In the real world, surfaces often have many layers of detail, with large-scale course features being further modified by smaller more subtle marks. You can simulate this by applying layers of noise at a range of frequencies as in Figure 26.6. This image was generated by Listing 26.5, which uses a loop to apply six layers of noise at increasingly high frequencies.

Listing 26.5 Layering noise.

```
float i;
float mag=0;
float freq=1;
```

```
for(i=0;i<6;i+=1)
    {
    mag+=(float noise(P*freq)-0.5)*2/freq;
    freq*=2;
    }
Ct=mag+0.5;
```

Figure 26.6 *Layering noise.*

The RenderMan noise function returns a value between 0 and 1 with an average of 0.5, but by subtracting 0.5 and multiplying by two we have scaled it to the range –1 to +1. In most applications of noise other than RenderMan, this is the normal form of noise used. We've used this modified form of noise as its average is 0, so that the average value of mag is not changed as more layers are added.

At each layer, the noise value is divided by frequency so that the higher frequency layers have a smaller amplitude than the courser ones. This construct is known as fractional Brownian motion, or more simply fBm, and is used frequently in shaders, as it closely models many structures found in nature. Simply using mag as a displacement, as in Listing 26.6, creates a dented appearance as in Figure 26.7.

Listing 26.6 fBm displacement.

```
displacement fbmDisp (
    float Km = 0.1;
    )
{
    vector NN = normalize(N);
    float i;
    float mag=0;
    float freq=1;

    for(i=0;i<6;i+=1)
        {
        mag+=(float noise(P*freq)-0.5)*2/freq;
        freq*=2.1;
        }

    mag /= length(vtransform("object",NN));

    P=P+mag*NN*Km;

    N=calculatenormal(P);
}
```

Figure 26.7 fBm displacement.

Turbulence

A function closely related to fBm is turbulence. This is very similar both in appearance and implementation, but has a more jagged look, as shown in Figure 26.8.

Figure 26.8 Turbulence.

Examining Listing 26.7 reveals that turbulence is almost exactly the same as fBm but uses the function abs() which takes the absolute value, ignoring the sign of the noise. This "folds" the noise creating a discontinuity that makes turbulence appear subtly different to fBm.

Listing 26.7 Turbulence.

```
float i;
float mag=0;
float freq=1;
for(i=0;i<6;i+=1)
    {
    mag+=abs(float noise(P*freq)-0.5)*2/freq;
```

```
      freq*=2;
      }
  Ct=mag;
```

You can control the exact nature of turbulence and fBm by reducing the number of layers, changing the difference in frequency between layers (known as the lacunarity), or by modifying the value by which each layer is scaled. A generic form of turbulence that incorporates these options as parameters is shown in Listing 26.8.

Listing 26.8 A more flexible turbulence.

```
surface turbulance (
        float layers=4;
        float startingFreq=4;
        float gain=1;
        float lacunarity=1.9132;
        string noiseSpace="shader";
        ...
        )
{
    ...

    float i;
    float mag=0;
    float freq=1;
    point PP=ptransform(noiseSpace,P);
    PP*=startingFreq;

    for(i=0;i<layers;i+=1)
        {
        mag+=abs(float noise(PP*freq)-0.5)
        *2/pow(freq,gain);
        freq*=lacunarity;
        }
    Ct=mag;

    ...
}
```

One common use of mag would be as the blend parameter of a mix(). You can also use it to blend between a greater range of colours using the spline function, which takes a variable number of colours (the minimum being four) and uses the first parameter to blend between them, as in Listing 26.9. By selecting the right set of colours this technique can be used to produce various rock textures such as marble (Figure 26.9), and flame like textures.

Listing 26.9 Using turbulence with a spline.

```
surface marble (
        float layers=4;
        float startingFreq=1;
        float gain=1;
        float lacunarity=1.9132;
        string noiseSpace="shader";
        float Ka = 1;
        float Kd = .5;
        float Ks = .5;
        float roughness = .1;
        color specularcolor = 1;
        float scale=0.04)
{
    normal Nf = faceforward (normalize(N),I);
    vector V = -normalize(I);
    color Ct;
    float i;
    float mag=0;
    float freq=startingFreq;
    point PP=ptransform(noiseSpace,P);
    PP*=scale;

    for(i=0;i<layers;i+=1)
        {
        mag+=abs(float noise(PP*freq)-0.5)*2/freq;
        freq*=lacunarity;
        }

    mag=smoothstep(0,0.4,mag);

    Ct=spline(mag,
    color "rgb" (0.25,0.35,0.25),
    color "rgb" (0.25,0.35,0.25),
    color "rgb" (0.20,0.30,0.20),
    color "rgb" (0.20,0.30,0.20),
    color "rgb" (0.20,0.30,0.20),
```

```
    color "rgb" (0.25,0.35,0.35),
    color "rgb" (0.25,0.35,0.35),
    color "rgb" (0.15,0.25,0.10),
    color "rgb" (0.15,0.25,0.10),
    color "rgb" (0.10,0.20,0.10),
    color "rgb" (0.10,0.20,0.10),
    color "rgb" (0.25,0.35,0.25),
    color "rgb" (0.10,0.10,0.20)
    );


    Oi = Os;
    Ci = Oi * ( Ct * (Ka*ambient() + Kd*diffuse(Nf)) +
               specularcolor * Ks*specular(Nf,V,roughness));
}
```

Figure 26.9 *Using turbulence with a spline (also Plate VI).*

Suggested activities

Try mixing noise into your shaders to give them a more organic feeling. Use noise both to modify the surface colour, and to modify texture coordinates. Try using noise to distort texture maps.

View noise at a range of frequencies – you should probably include an option to set the base frequency as a parameter to your shaders. Try layering noise as both fBm and turbulence, varying the gain and lacunarity parameters to generate different effects.

Summary

```
float noise(float);
float noise(float,float);
float noise(point);
float noise(point,float);
colour noise(float);
colour noise(float,float);
colour noise(point);
colour noise(point,float);
vector noise(float);
vector noise(float,float);
vector noise(point);
vector noise(point,float);
spline(t,color,color,color,color,color...);
```

Related functions

pnoise()

Some implementations of RenderMan also support a periodic noise, pnoise(), which repeats periodically, making it useful for surfaces which wrap, as it ensures the edges will join up perfectly.

Chapter

27

Aliasing

Introduction

When an object is viewed from further away, in the real world the surface detail will become blurred. Unless great care is taken, however, a computer-generated scene will produce unpredictable and ugly results when it contains details that are too small to be fully represented on the screen. This effect, known as "aliasing", is a constant problem for all rendering systems. In this section we'll look at some techniques you can use in your shaders to try and manage the problem.

What is aliasing?

We've so far considered shaders as describing a point on the surface, and assumed that the renderer will correctly reconstruct the surface from these points. While this model is adequate for many purposes it falls down when the features we are trying to describe on the surface become so small that they fall between the points that the renderer has picked. Figure 27.1 shows the results of this on the checkerboard shader we wrote in Chapter 22. Even at low frequencies the edges of the squares appear ragged, but as the checkerboard pattern becomes finer, the results become very ugly. In certain cases the high frequency pattern can even appear to be of a much lower frequency. This is a problem known as "aliasing".

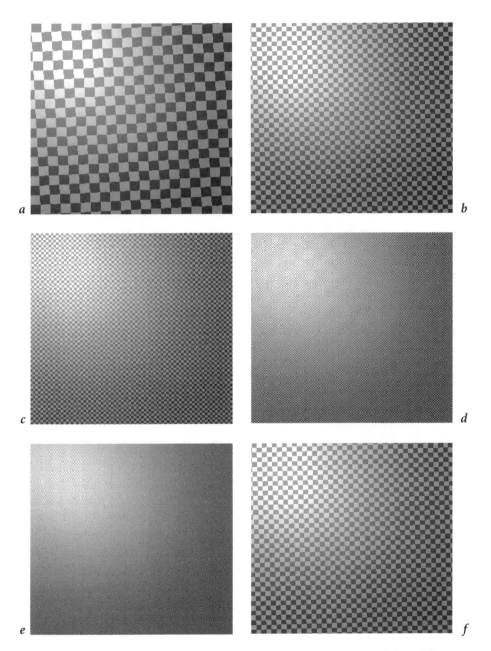

Figure 27.1 *Aliasing of the checkerboard shader:* repeatCount = *(a)* 20; *(b)* 40; *(c)* 80; *(d)* 160; *(e)* 320; *(f)* 640.

These artifacts become an even greater problem if you attempt to use the shader in an animation, as they will jump and flicker from frame to frame. Increasing PixelSamples, and reducing ShadingRate in the RIB file can help by instructing the renderer to use more points, but ultimately, no matter how close together the sampled points are, some features may fall between them.

Rather than considering the shader as describing a collection of points, it is necessary to consider the process of shading as operating on a grid of small squares. In PRMan these are known as micro-polygons. When the colour of the surface is changing slowly then a point sample is a good approximation to the average colour, but if there is too much fine detail (perhaps simply because the camera has moved away from the object) then the approximation will be poor, and the resulting image will suffer from sampling artifacts. Rather than calculating the surface colour at a single point the shader should be written to calculate the average colour of the square.

Softening edges

One of the most common ways in which fine detail can be inadvertently introduced into an image is simply by having a sharp edge. If the shader is written to calculate its result at only a single point it will fail to represent any square which spans the sharp edge correctly. A square which should be 50 per cent in and 50 per cent out of a region will be shaded as completely in or out depending on where the sampling point falls. We've already come across this problem and addressed it by avoiding the use of an "if" statement, and instead using a smoothstep function.

Smoothstep doesn't calculate the exact proportion of the square that falls on either side of the transition. Instead it replaces the sharp transition with a more gentle transition such that the point samples can change slowly from being inside to being outside. A point in the middle of the transition will correctly return 0.5, as if it were a square partially overlapping the two regions.

Previously we've used a variable "fuzz" to define the width of the transition region. A large value of fuzz should avoid aliasing but will produce a soft transition which results in a blurring of the surface detail. The alternative to using a small value of fuzz avoids this blurring but may reintroduce aliasing. While it is perfectly reasonable to hand tune fuzz for a few frames, if the shader needs to operate correctly at a range of resolutions we need to find an automatic mechanism for generating an appropriate value for fuzz.

The information we need to calculate fuzz is provided by the surface coordinates u and v. These are very similar to s and t but are locked to the surface rather than being user defined. The position of the current point sample is determined by u, v while the distance between the point samples is stored in the variables du and dv. For example, if u=0.5 and du=0.1 then the next sample point will have u=0.6. The shader therefore needs to consider a square from u, v to u+du, v+dv, as illustrated in Figure 27.2.

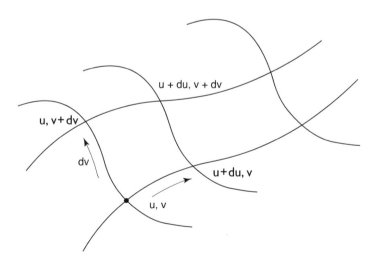

Figure 27.2 u, v *and* du, dv.

Though we now know the area we need to consider in terms of u and v, our texture is probably written in terms of ss and tt. The way that any variable changes across the surface can be found using the functions Du() and Dv(). The value returned by Du(ss) approximates how quickly ss is changing in the u-direction – technically known as the partial derivative. The difference between ss at the current point and ss at the next point can therefore be approximated using Du(ss)*du. Ss might also be changing in the v direction, so we arrive at an approximation for "fuzz" (which we'll now call filterWidth) by adding together the magnitude of the changes in the two directions.

The code to do this is used in Listing 27.1. Here we've used filterWidth in a shader that uses a sharp step in the top part of the object, and a smoothstep in the lower part, to make the difference clear. Calculating filterWidth like this produces a near optimal value of fuzz for the smoothstep. We therefore get a transition that is both sharp and alias free (Figure 27.3). If the object were to be re-rendered at a higher resolution, or you moved the object to be a different size on the screen then filterWidth should automatically adapt.

Listing 27.1 Automatically calculating fuzz.

```
float filterWidth;

    float ss=s+0.1*t;
    filterWidth=abs(Du(ss)*du)+abs(Dv(ss)*dv);

    if(t>0.5)
    {
        if(ss>0.5)
            Ct=color "rgb" (0,1,0);
        else
            Ct=Cs;
    }
    else
    {
        float onRight;
        onRight=smoothstep(0.5-filterWidth,
        0.5+filterWidth,ss);
        Ct=mix(Cs,color "rgb" (0,1,0),onRight);
    }
```

Figure 27.3 Automatically calculating fuzz.

Analytical anti-aliasing

As we now know the start and end of the region we're shading and we know the function in between, we should be able to work out the average value over that area. Point sampling provides the most basic approximation.

Consider the simple cosine function shown in Figure 27.4. Provided that we sample it at least twice in each cycle then the approximation of point sampling is reasonably accurate. However, if the frequency of the wave were to increase then the point samples become a poor fit to the actual signal. To remain accurate we would need to take the point samples closer together. The more samples we take, the better fit we obtain.

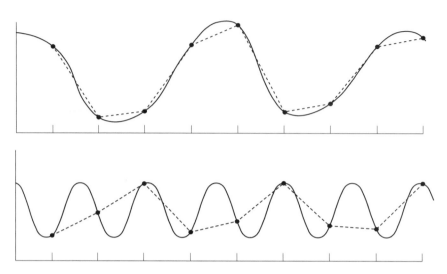

***Figure 27.4** Sampling Cos(ss).*

Theoretically if we could take an infinite number of samples, then the results would be accurate no matter how the input signal changed. It is exactly this kind of problem for which the branch of mathematics known as calculus was developed. If we know the original function, and can integrate it across the area of the micro-polygon then we can accurately reconstruct the function.

To correctly anti-alias the cos function we therefore need to evaluate

$$\int_{ss}^{ss+fw} \cos(x)dx$$

The integral of cosine is sine and hence the definite integral over this region is:

$$[\sin(x)]_{x=ss}^{s+fw} = \sin(ss + fw) - \sin(ss)$$

You should then divide this by the width to find the average value over this region:

$$val = \frac{\sin(ss + fw) - \sin(ss)}{fw}$$

Shader code to implement this is shown in Listing 27.2. When ss changes slowly the integrated version of the shader will appear exactly the same as `cos(ss)`, but at higher frequencies the samples of `cos(ss)` will become effectively random (or worse), while the integrated version will fade to a single uniform colour, as shown in Figure 27.5.

Listing 27.2 Point sampling versus anti-aliasing.

```
float ss=s*scale;
float filterWidth=abs(Du(ss)*du)+abs(Dv(ss)*dv);

if(s>0.5)
{
    val=cos(ss);
}
else
{
    val=(sin(ss+filterWidth)-sin(ss))
        /filterWidth;
}

Ct=val*0.5+0.5;
```

Figure 27.5 Point sampling versus anti-aliasing.

The left-hand side of the image in Figure 27.5 shows four regions of increasing frequency which have been correctly anti-aliased. The low frequency at the bottom is clearly visible while at the top left the detailing is so fine that it has correctly blurred out to uniform colour. The right side of the image simply uses point sampling, and as the frequency increases the results become inaccurate, eventually producing a completely erroneous image.

Integrating 2D functions

So far we've considered a function of only one variable, but more often we have a function that varies in both s and t. When we apply integration to a function of more than one variable, the maths becomes slighly more complex and obscure, as we need to use "vector calculus". Typically, to integrate over a 2D area we have to solve a double integral. For example, in the case of the function sin(ss)*sin(tt) we need to evaluate:

$$\int_{ss}^{ss+sFw} \int_{tt}^{tt+tFw} \sin(x)\sin(y)dydx$$

This is handled first by integrating with respect to y while considering x to be a constant, giving:

$$\int_{ss}^{ss+sFw} \sin(x)[-\cos(y)]_{y=tt}^{tt+tFw} dx$$

and then integrating again, this time with respect to ss while tt remains constant. If we solve this, and divide by the area of the micro-polygon we arrive at:

$$val = \frac{(\cos(ss) - \cos(ss+sFw))(\cos(tt) - \cos(tt+tFw))}{sFwtFw}$$

which is the average value of the function over the micropolygon.

Once you've gone through this procedure for a real case you'll discover that the cases we've tacked here are in fact particularly simple, and it is generally even more difficult.

The real problem is that while you might think that once you've integrated each function in your shader your aliasing problems are solved, this simply isn't the case. While a solution may be available for most individual functions, when several functions are used together (known as composition), you can't simply combine the integrals! More formally, if

$$A(x) = \int a(x)dx$$

and

$$B(x) = \int b(x)dx$$

then, in the general case

$$A(B(x)) \neq \int a(b(x))dx$$

We should really be integrating the entire shader, including the lighting models (a particular source of aliasing for displacement shaders) as a single function. Fortunately all is not lost – we're only interested in the appearance of our objects after all, and in many cases integrating one or more "troublesome" functions within your shader can produce dramatic improvements.

Frequency clamping

Even for experienced shader writers with a strong mathematical background, analytically anti-aliasing can be very difficult, or even impossible in many cases. However, many functions have an average value that can be used when viewed from a great distance. When examined at closer range point sampling is adequate. We can therefore simply blend between these two values at the point where the function starts to alias.

If we consider `noise()` then it has a feature size of about 1 – that is, to get a reasonable approximation to the `noise()` function the filter width would need to be less than approximately 0.5. We can use this knowledge to produce a noise texture that shouldn't alias, as in Listing 27.3. When the filter width is less than 0.2 we have many samples, so the normal value of noise is perfectly adequate. If the filter width is greater than 0.6 then the average value of 0.5 is used. Between these two ranges the noise is faded out gradually.

Listing 27.3 Frequency clamped noise.

```
float filterWidth=abs(Du(ss)*du)+abs(Dv(ss)*dv);
float val;

float fade=smoothstep(0.2,0.6,filterWidth);
val=(1-fade)*(float noise(ss))+fade*0.5;

Ct=val;
```

This approach is commonly used with fBm, as shown in Listing 27.4. Here we've calculated the noise function based on both ss and tt, so we need to calculate a filter width in both directions, and fade out the noise based on the largest filter. Rather than recalculating filter width each time round the loop, we simply increase the filter width by freq, generating the same result.

Listing 27.4 Frequency clamped fBm.

```
float i;
float freq=1;
float mag=0;
float filterWidthSS=abs(Du(ss)*du)+abs(Dv(ss)*dv);
float filterWidthTT=abs(Du(tt)*du)+abs(Dv(tt)*dv);
float filterWidth=filterWidthSS>filterWidthTT?
                        filterWidthSS:filterWidthTT;

for(i=0;i<6;i+=1)
{
    float val;
    float fade=smoothstep(0.2,0.6,filterWidth*freq);
    val=(1-fade)*(float noise(ss*freq,tt*freq))
    +fade*0.5;

    mag+=(val-0.5)/freq;
    freq *=2;
}

Ct=mag+0.5;
```

Examining the results of this shader on the left-hand side of Figure 27.6 you can see that even at low frequencies the anti-aliased version is a little softer than the point sampled implementation on the right, while at high frequencies the point sampled version is simply random noise.

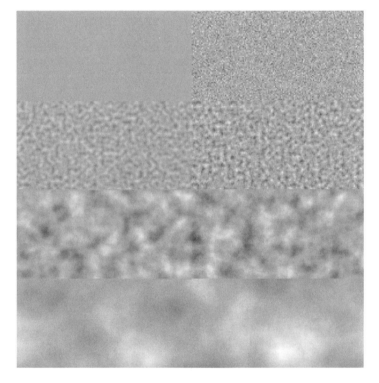

Figure 27.6 Frequency clamped fBm.

Checkerboard

While the principles of anti-aliasing are relatively straightforward, actually applying them in practice is somewhat more difficult. We'll therefore attempt to create a checkerboard, similar to the one we've previously constructed, but avoiding the aliasing problems from which that suffers.

To anti-alias the checkerboard, we need to consider two aspects – first, we need to soften the edges of the squares, by using smoothstep. Secondly, we need to consider the case where the squares are too small to be adequately represented, and hence we will use frequency clamping to fade the board to a mid-grey.

If we decide that each square is one unit wide in ss and one unit high in tt, then we need to consider the range 0–2 to generate a complete cycle. We'll therefore use mod to create a 2 by 2 tile. Considering one direction at a time, the obvious thing to do would be to transition from black to white at one and back to black again at two. This places the transitions at the edges of our 2 by 2 tile, however, which may be inconvenient. Instead, at approximately 0.5, we transition from black to white and at 1.5 we transition from white to back. This can be done using the code in Listing 27.5, which generates a set of vertical stripes as in Figure 27.7. By duplication of this code in tt we could generate horizontal stripes.

Listing 27.5 Vertical stripes.

```
color Ct;

float repeatCount=40;
float ss=s*repeatCount+t;
float filterWidthSS=abs(Du(ss)*du)+abs(Dv(ss)*dv);
float smag;

ss=mod(ss,2);
smag =smoothstep(0.5-filterWidthSS,
      0.5+filterWidthSS,ss);
smag-=smoothstep(1.5-filterWidthSS,
      1.5+filterWidthSS,ss);

Ct=smag;
```

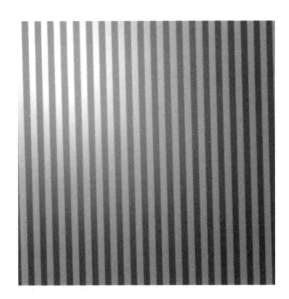

Figure 27.7 Vertical stripes.

In Listing 27.6 we combine these horizontal and vertical stripes into squares. To do this we need to scale smag and tmag into the range -1 to +1, multiply them together, and then scale back into the standard 0-1 range. By doing this we get a check pattern, as in Figure 27.8. This works because when smag and tmag are the same we get a white square, while if they're different we get a black square – an operation known as an Exclusive OR (Figure 27.9).

Listing 27.6 A basic checkerboard.

```
float filterWidthSS=abs(Du(ss)*du)+abs(Dv(ss)*dv);
float filterWidthTT=abs(Du(tt)*du)+abs(Dv(tt)*dv);
float smag,tmag;

ss=mod(ss,2);
tt=mod(tt,2);
smag =smoothstep(0.5-
filterWidthSS,0.5+filterWidthSS,ss);
smag-=smoothstep(1.5-
filterWidthSS,1.5+filterWidthSS,ss);
smag=smag*2-1;
```

```
tmag =smoothstep(0.5-
filterWidthTT,0.5+filterWidthTT,tt);
tmag-=smoothstep(1.5-
filterWidthTT,1.5+filterWidthTT,tt);
tmag=tmag*2-1;

Ct=(smag*tmag)/2+0.5;
```

Figure 27.8 *A basic checkerboard.*

-1	*	-1	=	1
-1	*	1	=	-1
1	*	-1	=	-1
1	*	1	=	1

Figure 27.9 *An Exclusive OR function.*

We now need to consider how the pattern will fade out as filter width increases. Previously we used the worst case filter width from the ss and tt directions, but here we can filter each separately. This is a better approach as, due to the orientation of the object or the choice of different scales in the s and t directions, the filter widths might not be the same.

One complete cycle of the stripes has a width of two and hence we must have a filter width of less than one to accurately reproduce them. We therefore fade smag and tmag to their mid-value before combining them. The resultant shader is shown in Listing 27.7.

Listing 27.7 The completed checkerboard.

```
surface check  (
    float  Ka = 1;
    float  Kd = .5;
    float  Ks = .5;
    float  roughness = .1;
    color  specularcolor = 1;)
{

    normal  Nf = faceforward (normalize(N),I);
    vector  V = -normalize(I);
    color  Ct;

    float  repeatCount=40;
    float  ss=s*repeatCount+t;
    float  tt=t*repeatCount-s;
    float  filterWidthSS=abs(Du(ss)*du)+abs(Dv(ss)*dv);
    float  filterWidthTT=abs(Du(tt)*du)+abs(Dv(tt)*dv);
    float  smag,tmag;

    ss=mod(ss,2);
    tt=mod(tt,2);

    smag =smoothstep(0.5-filterWidthSS,
    0.5+filterWidthSS,ss);
    smag-=smoothstep(1.5-filterWidthSS,
    1.5+filterWidthSS,ss);
    smag=smag*2-1;
    smag*=1-smoothstep(0.4,1.2,filterWidthSS);

    tmag =smoothstep(0.5-filterWidthTT,
```

```
0.5+filterWidthTT,tt);
tmag-=smoothstep(1.5-filterWidthTT,
1.5+filterWidthTT,tt);
tmag=tmag*2-1;
tmag*=1-smoothstep(0.4,1.2,filterWidthTT);


Ct=(smag*tmag)/2+0.5;

Oi = Os;
Ci = Oi * ( Ct * (Ka*ambient() + Kd*diffuse(Nf)) +
    specularcolor * Ks*specular(Nf,V,roughness));
}
```

Suggested activities

Modify your shaders to automatically calculate their own filter widths for any smoothsteps you have used. Investigate the effect of this upon the images produced.

Examine your shaders for other examples of aliasing. Consider if it is possible to reduce the problem using either an analytical or frequency clamping approach.

It is also possible to anti-alias the checkerboard shader analytically. Consider how this might be done.

Summary and further information

Anti-aliasing is an on-going problem to which there are no simple answers. In every shader a trade off must be made between the quality of the final image, the range of shots for which the shader will be viable, the shader development time, and the render time.

Chapter 28

Shading Models

Introduction

In many cases the standard plastic-like shading model will suffice, at least during initial shader development. As you progress, however, you'll wish to refine the way light interacts with your surface. RenderMan allows you to interrogate each of the lights in the scene, and hence shade your surface in any way you feel is appropriate.

Inside the standard models

The diffuse and specular functions typically used to calculate the shading of a surface collect the light from all of the light sources within the scene and, for each one, work out how much will be reflected towards the camera. While having this process automated for us is very convenient, if you need to create new lighting models – for example, an anisotropic surface which reflects light only in certain directions – then it is necessary to break open these functions and implement them manually.

Diffuse

The standard diffuse model is defined such that the contribution from each light is:

```
Cl*normalize(L).normalize(N)
```

That is, the colour of the light multiplied by the dot product of the incident light vector and the surface normal. To turn this into useful code we need to put this inside a loop that visits each light in turn. This is done in Listing 28.1. Illuminance is a looping construct unique to SL, which loops over all of the lights in the scene that are visible from the point being shaded.

Listing 28.1 Diffuse `Illuminance` model.

```
color Cdiff=0;

illuminance(P,Nf,PI/2)
{
    Cdiff+=Cl*normalize(L).Nf;
}
```

The three parameters to `Illuminance` are the point being shaded, the direction of interest and an angle. These three variables form a cone, as shown in Figure 28.1. Any lights outside this cone are excluded from the loop. Within the loop, the new global variables `Cl` and `L` are set up representing the colour of the light, and a vector from the surface to the light source. We simply need to apply the lighting model of our choice and add that to the total light recorded so far.

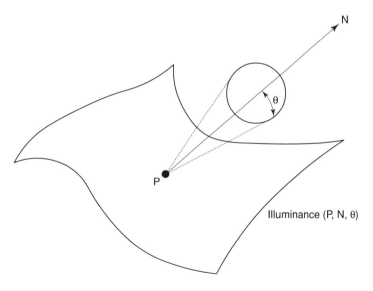

Figure 28.1 *The parameters to* `Illuminance`.

In this case we've used `Cl` and `L` in a diffuse lighting model, which results in a value of `Cdiff` identical to that returned by the standard diffuse function.

Specular

Similarly, we can build our own specular function as shown in Listing 28.2. This uses vector H, which is half way between the observer vector V and the direction to the light L. We take the dot product of this and the surface normal to get a value that falls off as we move away from the mirror angle. This is then raised to a power to control the size of the specular highlight.

Listing 28.2 Specular Illuminance model.

```
color Cspec=0;

illuminance(P,Nf,PI/2)
{
Vector H = normalize (V + normalize(L));
Cspec+ = Cl*pow(H.Nf,1/roughness);
}
```

This lighting model is equivalent to the official RenderMan specular function, but may not correspond to the highlights produced by a particular renderer, as many use slightly different code to produce highlights which are subjectively more pleasing.

Custom illumination models

Since the orientation for the surface and the direction of each incident light is known, you can combine these together in any way you see fit, to produce the lighting model of your choice. You could start with a physical model of how light interacts with a surface and try and implement it, or simply tweak one of the existing models to produce something that looks good.

One interesting group of illumination models are known as anisotropic. Whereas most surfaces reflect light equally in all orientations, some, such as a vinyl record or compact disc, reflect light in a highly directional way. This is usually due to some fine detail such as the record's grooves which would be too small to actually render directly but have a major effect on the surface's appearance.

To create such a surface we need to factor the orientation of the surface coordinates into the lighting model. For example, consider a surface made from highly reflective threads like satin. To recreate such a surface you would need to consider how the incident light is oriented to these threads rather than to the surface normal.

If we assume that the threads run in the u direction then we can find the direction of the threads in 3D space using `Du(P)`. If we normalize `Du(P)` and take the dot product with H (as in the standard specular function) we would get a lighting model which was brightest when the light was shining along the threads. In fact we want to maximize the highlight when the H is at 90 degrees to the thread, and hence we use a scale factor of:

```
sqrt(1-pow(H.dir,2)
```

This lighting model is used as part of the shader in Listing 28.3, which also includes ambient and diffuse components. Note how the highlights are stretched along the surface when this is applied to the teapot model in Figure 28.2 (also Plate VI). Figure 28.3 (also Plate VI) shows the result of applying an identical shader, but with the threads oriented in the *v* direction.

Listing 28.3 An anisotropic surface.

```
surface satinU (
        float roughness = 0.1;
        color specularcolor = 1;)
{
    normal Nf = faceforward (normalize(N),I);
    vector V = -normalize(I);
    color Caniso=0;
    vector dir=normalize(Du(P));

    illuminance(P,Nf,PI/2)
        {
        vector H=normalize(normalize(V)+normalize(L));
        float scale=sqrt(1-(H.dir*H.dir));
```

```
        Caniso+=Cl*pow(scale,1/roughness);
        }

    Oi = Os;
    Ci = Os * (Caniso+Cs*(ambient()+0.2*diffuse(Nf)));
}
```

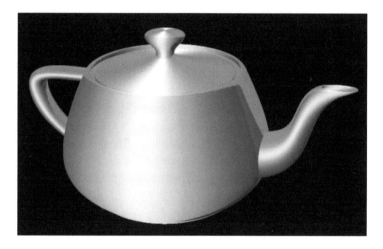

Figure 28.2 *An anisotropic surface* (also Plate VI).

Figure 28.3 *Reorienting the satin shader* (also Plate VI).

Suggested activities

Consider whether any of your shaders could be improved by a more complex lighting model. Try creating your own illumination model, either realistic or completely fake.

Modify the satin code into a shader that has a parameter allowing the orientation to be set. Apply this to a model like the teapot, orienting the shader for maximum effect on each part of the object.

The code for a large range of illumination models is available in various shaders which are available on the Internet. Try merging some of these into your own shaders.

Summary

```
illuminance(P,dir,theta) { ... }
```
Cl - colour of the incident light
L - direction of incident light.

Chapter

29

Other Kinds of Shader

Introduction

So far we've concentrated on surface shaders as these are by far the most common. However, RenderMan also allows shaders to control other parts of the rendering process. In this chapter you'll see how light shaders can be used to define the behaviour of lights, while a volume shader can modify the observed colour of a surface due to atmospheric effects such as fog.

Volume shaders

Sometimes the images we see are not the simple result of light bouncing from hard surfaces. Often the light is modified in some way as it passes through the air, perhaps by smoke or fog. To describe the properties of the space through which light travels, RenderMan provides volume shaders.

The typical use of a volume shader is to describe the effect of the atmosphere in modifying the colour of a surface after it has been calculated by the surface shader, but before it reaches the camera. When used in this way it is known as an "atmosphere". A volume shader therefore does its work by modifying Ci.

One of the simplest descriptions of an atmosphere would be to fade out objects beyond a certain point. We can do this by considering the length of I – the vector from the camera to the shaded point. If this is less than a certain distance then Ci should remain unchanged, beyond a second distance you should replace it with the background colour. In the mid region we blend the two together using mix and smoothstep, as shown in Listing 29.1 and Figure 29.1. As always, when dealing with vectors we should specify a coordinate space to ensure consistency between renderers.

Listing 29.1 A simple depth fade shader.

```
volume depthfade (
      float mindistance = 1, maxdistance = 9;
      color background = 0;)
{
    float d;
    vector Icam=vtransform("camera",I);
    d = smoothstep (mindistance, maxdistance,
    length(Icam));
    Ci = mix (Ci, background, d);
}
```

Figure 29.1 *A simple depth fade shader.*

A slightly more realistic effect would be to realize that as an object moves away through a foggy atmosphere, it becomes increasingly faint, but never disappears completely. This exponential effect is provided by the "fog" shader shown in Figure 29.2 and Listing 29.2.

Listing 29.2 A fog shader.

```
volume fog (
    float distance = 1;
    color background = 0;)
{
    vector Icam=vtransform("camera",I);
    float d = 1 - exp (-length(Icam)/distance);
    Ci = mix (Ci, background, d);
    Oi = mix (Oi, color(1,1,1), d);
}
```

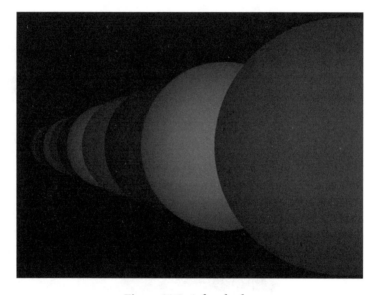

Figure 29.2 A fog shader.

Though these shaders are very simple, volume shaders can use all of the techniques available to regular shaders. You could, for example, examine the position of the point being shaded, and use that to define a layer of fog, rather than fogging the whole scene equally.

For maximum flexibility atmosphere shaders can be applied on a per object basis. Unless you're attempting something unusual, however, it is probably best to apply one atmosphere shader to the whole scene. You should also be aware that if there is no object covering a particular part of the image, then it will not be fogged. To avoid this strange effect, it is common to place a large sphere around the whole scene when atmosphere shaders are being used.

Light shaders

In addition to controlling the appearance of surfaces, you can also use shaders to control the light sources in your scene. While a surface shader's job is to calculate the observed colour of a surface, a light shader's job is to decide how much light a particular source casts upon a point.

Pointlights

The simplest interesting light shader is the pointlight source. The code for this is shown in Listing 29.3. A pointlight is defined by a position, an intensity and a colour, which are provided by parameters. From these the shader must calculate a value for Cl and L which will be passed to the surface shader for use in an illuminance loop, or one of the standard lighting functions.

Listing 29.3 A pointlight source.

```
light pointlight (
    float intensity = 1;
    color lightcolor = 1;
    point from = point "shader" (0,0,0);)
{
    illuminate (from)
        Cl = intensity * lightcolor / (L . L);
}
```

In most cases light shaders make use of an illuminate statement. This looks a lot like the illuminance loop we used to collect light in a surface shader. In the case of the pointlight source we tell illuminate the position of our light source. This automatically sets up L to be the vector from the light source's position to the surface. From this we calculate the colour of the light hitting the surface by multiplying the light's intensity by its colour. We divide by L.L, as this provides a natural fall-off in light intensity as can be seen in Figure 29.3, which shows the pointlight illuminating a flat surface.

Figure 29.3 A pointlight source.

Although the standard point and spotlight shaders exhibit a physically accurate illumination pattern, there is no reason why this need be the case. In fact non-physically realistic lights can be far easier to work with. As an example of this, in Listing 29.4 we've created a light that only casts light on surfaces which are between two and three units away. In addition it doesn't fall away as quickly. You could use such a shader to light an area in a more even fashion than the standard pointlight, as it avoids the extremes of light and dark. However, as can be seen in Figure 29.4, the lack of physical realism can make the scene harder to read.

Listing 29.4 A non-physical light.

```
light nearfarlight (
    float intensity = 1;
    color lightcolor = 1;
    float near = 2;
    float far = 3;
```

```
    point from = point "shader" (0,0,0);)
{
    float length;
    float brightness;

    illuminate (from)
        {
        length=sqrt(L.L);
        if(length<near || length>far)
            brightness=0;
        else
            brightness=1/length;
        Cl = intensity * lightcolor*brightness;
        }
}
```

Figure 29.4 *A non-physical light.*

Spotlights

A second form of illuminate statement allows you to specify not only a position for the light, but also a direction and a beam angle. Only those points within the cone will be illuminated. Not only is this an easy way to create a simple spotlight, it is also efficient, as it allows the renderer to skip the calculations for points which are not going to be lit.

Such an illuminate statement is used in Listing 29.5. Only points within 30 degrees of the light's axis are illuminated, creating the illumination pattern seen in Figure 29.5. While this shader does create a beam of light, the edges of that beam are sharp and unattractive. The standard spotlight incorporates additional code to smoothly transition between the area inside the beam and the areas that are not lit.

Listing 29.5 A conical beamlight.

```
light
beamlight ( float intensity = 1;
            color lightcolor = 1;
            point from = point "shader" (0,0,0);
            point to = point "shader" (0,0,1);
            )
{
    uniform vector A = normalize(to-from);

    illuminate (from, A, radians(30))
        {
        Cl = intensity * lightcolor/(L.L) ;
        }
}
```

Figure 29.5 A conical beam light.

Having created some basic light sources, you're free to modify the resultant light in any way you feel appropriate. For example, in Listing 29.6 we've used the angle between the axis and the L vector to modify the light's colour, producing the pattern of lighting seen in Figure 29.6.

Listing 29.6 Modifying a light's colour.

```
light colorlight (
      float intensity = 1;
      point from = point "shader" (0,0,0);
      point to = point "shader" (0,0,1);
      )
{
    float cosangle;
    color lightcolor = 1;
    uniform vector A = normalize(to-from);

    illuminate (from, A, radians(30))
        {
        cosangle=(L.A)/length(L);
        lightcolor=color "hsv" (cosangle*10,1,1);
        Cl = intensity * lightcolor/(L.L) ;
        }
}
```

Figure 29.6 *Modifying a light's colour.*

Shadows

One of the most common modifications is the addition of support for shadow maps. Having created a shadow map as described in Chapter 14, actually using it is remarkably simple. By simply passing the name of a map to the shadow function, as in Listing 29.7 you can obtain a value indicating to what extent a point is in shadow. Within a light shader `Ps` represents the point on the surface being lit, and hence `1-shadow("shadowmap",Ps)` calculates to what extent the point should be illuminated. This value is simply factored into the lighting calculation.

Listing 29.7 Creating a shadow.

```
light shadowlight (
    float intensity = 1;
    color lightcolor = 1;
    point from = point "shader" (0,0,0);
    point to = point "shader" (0,0,1);
    string mapname="";
    )
{
    float atten=1;
    uniform vector A = normalize(to-from);
```

```
illuminate (from, A, radians(30))
    {
    if(mapname != "")
        atten=1-shadow(mapname,Ps);
    Cl = atten*intensity * lightcolor/(L.L) ;
    }
}
```

Suggested activities

Try adding a subtle fog to some of your scenes.

The light in Listing 29.4 is prone to aliasing, as it creates sharp edges. Use smoothstep to reduce the problem.

Try incorporating texture maps, or adding noise into light shaders to create the effect of light passing through trees or other obstructions.

Summary

```
illuminate(P)
illuminate(P,A,angle)
shadow("mapname",P)
```

Related functions

solar(direction,angle)

Not all lights have a position. The solar statement serves a similar function to illuminate but does not require a position. It is used to create distant lights such as the sun.

Bibliography

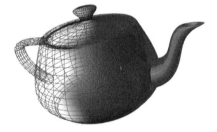

Essential reading

Four publications cover most of the information required to make successful use of a RenderMan renderer. Anyone seriously interested in rendering will eventually end up owning these books. They all assume a relatively high level of technical ability, and cover a lot of material very quickly. However, if you've worked your way through this book then you should be able to tackle them without too much difficulty.

RenderMan Companion: A Programmer's Guide to Realistic Computer Graphics, **Steve Upstill, Addison Wesley, 1990.**

For most RenderMan users this is the primary source of information. It covers modelling and shading in great detail. It is, however, based on the original RenderMan standard, and as such has a number of omissions. Most obviously the book was written before the introduction of RIB files, and hence discusses RenderMan purely in terms of the C API. While adapting the information to RIB is usually trivial, it does make the book difficult to follow for weaker programmers.

Advanced RenderMan, **A. Apodaca and L. Gritz, Morgan Kaufmann, 1999.**

This book starts at a simple level, and provides a moderately good reference section covering both RIB and Shading Language. It also includes a tutorial section covering much of the maths and physics of rendering. However, it moves quickly from this introduction to more complex topics. As such it does live up to its "Advanced" title.

The RenderMan Standard v3.2, Pixar, 2000.

This document, freely available as a PDF from Pixar's website (www.pixar.com), formally defines the RenderMan API including all the extensions and features added by Pixar up until the time of its publication. As such it provides a level of detail unmatched elsewhere, including details of features which are not supported even by Pixar's renderer. The price for this accuracy, however, is a text which few users would choose to read. If you need to know exactly how something works then this is the place to look, but for most purposes refer to the previous texts.

Texturing and Modelling: A Procedural Approach, D.S. Ebert, F.K. Musgrave, D. Peachey, K. Perlin and S. Worley (eds.), Academic Press, 1998.

This is not a book about RenderMan as such, but a broader guide to the concepts of procedural texturing. However, most of the ideas can be implemented in SL, or are already built into the language. The format of the book is a collection of chapters written by a number of authors, which makes it a little inconsistent at times, and the academic style may seem off putting, but the quality of information makes this an essential book which you'll return to many times.

Index

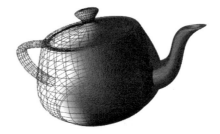